DESIGN
FOR UTOPIA

DESIGN FOR UTOPIA

Selected Writings of Charles Fourier

With an Introduction by
CHARLES GIDE

New Foreword by
FRANK E. MANUEL

Translated by
JULIA FRANKLIN

SCHOCKEN BOOKS • NEW YORK

Studies in the Libertarian and Utopian Tradition
First published in 1901 with the title
Selections from the Writings of Fourier
First SCHOCKEN edition 1971
Second Printing, 1976
Introduction copyright © 1971 by Schocken Books Inc.
Library of Congress Catalog Card No. 70-148712
Manufactured in the United States of America

CONTENTS

Contents

DESIGN
FOR UTOPIA

FOREWORD
Fourier Redivivus

FROM a constricted, monotonous existence that nearly suffocated him, Fourier the underpaid clerk, roomer in dreary boarding houses, escaped into a rich and variegated world of fantasy. Rancor against a repressive hypocritical society that crushed human nature, that condemned him and his fellow creatures of every social class to impoverishment, gave birth to vengeful images of the collapse of "Civilization" and to visions of extravagant plenitude that he wove into a doctrine of gratification, harmony, and joy. He called it a system of passionate attraction.

In 1808, at the height of the Napoleonic victories, Fourier foretold the doom. The most frightful prospects were in store, he threatened, unless men were prepared to follow him in establishing a new society founded on the emancipation of the passions and proclaiming the triumph of sensual pleasure. He saw this liberation as the only antidote to savage competition and ceaseless political turmoil. A sexual revolution was not a prolegomenon to—as Wilhelm Reich would contend in the Germany of the 1920's—but a preventive of political upheaval. Financially ruined by the Revolution of 1789 and its aftermath, Fourier abominated its name and castigated the rationalist *philosophes* and their heirs the social scientists for shortsightedness, Europocentrism, and transgressions against nature. In his new society, even the humblest would be guaranteed such fulfillment in love and occupational relationships, that they would become ardently attached to their work, instead of sinking into indolence and brigandage. Men cared nothing for juridical rights or engineering gadgets but yearned to express freely their different passionate natures, to enjoy to the limit the pleasures of bed and table, to indulge their appetites, gross and sublimated. In Fourier's history of sensate progression, the ascetics, moralists, and rationalists were the sinners, the libertines the new saints. A recently published manuscript of his, for the most part a reiteration of his printed writings, was called *The New World of Love*.

"Civilization" was a pejorative term that signified a dastardly violation of Nature's designs. Fourier indicted his society for a gratification lag: for three thousand years the productive capacity of the civilized world had already been sufficiently developed to meet all the desires of men; in that period satisfactions for rich and poor alike had not advanced one jot, for all the trumpeted progress of the arts and sciences. Love was stunted by legalized monogamy or adulterous affairs, and created anguish instead of pleasure; work was an enslavement. With an acid-dipped pen Fourier depicted "civilized" man in all his anxious discontents, consumed with unappeased appetites amid opulence. Boredom was the fate of man in the civilized state—"less rich with what he owns than poor with what he has not."

Inevitably wrath was building up against this condition. To forestall another holocaust it was urgent that Civilization abdicate in favor of the next stage of history, Harmony, a yea-saying world of "phalansteries," where all possible psychological types would be cherished, all longings given heed. Fourier envisaged the glorification of the senses in a society responsive to the particular desires, predilections, and capacities of its constituent members. With solemn scientificism he calculated that a unit of some 2000 persons would yield the diversity of temperaments, 810 in all (with male and female variants), required for carrying out the functions of society. While all persons in phalanstery would attain full gratification, their differing propensities and aptitudes would be specially nurtured. In this way the development and expression of individual passions would promote collective ends. Fourier's ideal calls to mind the "synergic" society originated by Ruth Benedict and expounded by Abraham H. Maslow, who found it consonant with his own doctrine of self-actualization. In synergy, as Maslow defined it, the individual acting in his own behalf at the same time furthers social ends, fulfilling simultaneously and harmoniously his obligations to himself and his responsibilities to society. In Fourier the mechanism for achieving a synergic phalanstery involved a kind of natural shuffling or shaking down of large, random agglomerations to produce all the essential psychic types and an overall passion for "unityism"—today we might say community—that would integrate individual with group happiness.

Fourier's dream was universalist. He inveighed against the reformers and moralists preoccupied only with their own continent or a mere corner of it. A reorganized society would be coterminous with the globe. His emancipation proclamation addressed itself to all races and classes of humankind—women as well as men, toddlers and the elderly. The needs of one and the needs of all would be encompassed. If means were devised to satisfy old men lusting after maidens, dowagers smitten with the charms of youths were granted their pleasures, too. Even the pain of an occasional amorous rejection would be assuaged by a sacerdotal corps of lovers. Fourier did not allow his own antipathy to children to cloud his recognition of their particular needs: the educational system in phalanstery was permissive, and tasks reserved for children made the most of their passion for wallowing in filth.

Life in phalanstery was dedicated to the passions rampant, catalogued by Fourier's orderly, obsessive mind as sensory, affective, and serial. His probing of the human psyche led him to identify and include a cabalist passion for intrigue and a butterfly passion for change and variety. All the passions would be discharged into wholesome channels or act in concert with complementary passions to achieve ends salutary for the whole society. The erotic was central to this new world. It was not merely an embellishment of life, a crown to man's happiness—it suffused all of existence. Unrepressed sexuality, pervading relationships of love and labor, would regenerate the human race, now decaying in fraud, deprivation, and odious, unremitting toil.

Perhaps through introspecting about the frustration that bred his own destructive fantasies—he threatened Frenchmen with a wholesale carnage in which millions would die unless they ac-

cepted his doctrine—this self-revealed man formulated a theory
of what we would now call repression. When passions were stifled
they generated counterpassions. If desires were choked, energies
would erupt wildly to menace the individual himself and the rest
of society. In Fourier's system there would be no need to outlaw
monsters like the Marquis de Sade; they would simply evaporate
in gratification.

Fourier rhapsodized over the future of the senses in Harmony.
Gormandism, he predicted, would be the "magnetic needle" of
health and wisdom, leading a man to satisfy his own and the
desires of others, transforming itself into the science of gas-
trosophy, whose most skillful practitioners would be revered as
oracles and saints. So with olefactory and other satisfactions, provided in ample measure to reverse the sensuous poverty and
shriveling of the great mass of mankind. Fourier's dreams of delight were by no means limited to gustatory and erotic enjoyments. By encouraging a variety of natural talents, the phalansteries would attain to a brilliant apogee in the arts, sciences, and
entertainments. This lonely bachelor who had sampled the contemptible fare of the provinces during long trips as a traveling
salesman took sweet revenge in contrasting their shabby spec-
tacles with the veritable banquet of concerts, dramas, dances that
would be set before the poorest of phalansterians by local per-
formers and wandering bands of troubadors, male and female.

Thus, Fourier's answer to the profound dislocations and harsh
stringencies of bourgeois industrial society was based on a won-
drously imaginative conception of expanded human needs and
limitless potentialities. Though his system was geared primarily to
sensate and sensual needs, he grudgingly made allowance for the
rationalist virtuosity of his archfoes, the moralizing professors
of natural law, letting them produce parodies of their own works
for the delectation of the phalansteries. So much for loathsome
Reason. The psychophysical makeup of each individual was extremely complex and comprised an intricate web of sexual and
social requirements. If there is an implied hierarchy of values
among them, the rare and more esoteric needs are prized above
the common ones. The phalanstery would seek out these extra-

ordinary specimens, cultivate them, and search even throughout the world for their precise complement in other persons. Though in his published works Fourier avoided discussion of homosexuality, his manuscripts rank it along with other sexual preferences. The needs of the phalansterians are continually changing in the course of a single day and in the successive stages of the life cycle. Though numerous, they are categorizable by types and manipulable with the aid of a central archive where each person's profile of needs is on record. Computerized pairing and selection were not yet anticipated, but their equivalent was approximated on a manual basis. A capacity to maintain multiple and varied relationships, to lead a full, complicated life of the senses, was highly appreciated, as was the gift for pleasing others through artistic creations. The excitement of novelty, of rich sensate experience, permeated phalanstery and imparted a vibrant quality to all its activities.

Fourier's merciless dissection of bourgeois morality—no less a knower than Balzac admired his analysis of fifty-odd types of cuckoldry—and his utopia of endless stimulation and fulsome pleasure, from which boredom would be forever banished, were too far-out to be accepted unblinkingly even by his own disciples. They tended to stress his organization of cooperative work relations and neglect his sexual doctrines. Fourier's ideas on productive labor were the primary focus of Professor Charles Gide, who once introduced this collection to respectable readers. To socialist and communist thinkers of the Victorian age Fourierism was downright abhorrent—in Karl Marx it evoked images of the brothel. Some of Fourier's manuscripts were not published until the 1960's, when there was a recrudescence of interest in a utopia of immediate, uninhibited satisfaction of psychophysical needs, and Fourierist phrases began to crop up in the writings of contemporary theorists. André Breton had hailed him as a great emancipator of the senses. Herbert Marcuse foresaw the sexual impulses renewed and fortified to the point where they would eroticize all relationships. Bits of Fourier chirp through Marcuse's theory of a new rationality of gratification, creating its own division of labor, priorities, hierarchy. Erich Fromm, too, seems to hark back wistfully to Fourierism when he regrets the lack of free labor in companionship and love that could have been ensured by a "humanistic socialism." Norman Brown, whose apoliticism brings him even closer to Fourier, preaches a childlike immersion in the polymorphous pleasures of the body as the prelude to a new and happy age of play or "attractive work."

And so a paradox has evolved: Fourier prophet of love and champion of the flesh redeemed has become the spiritual father of those he execrated—fashionable moralists, academic philosophers, even revolutionaries. Fourier's is a magnificent version of the Cockaigne and Adamite utopias that have possessed segments of mankind from time immemorial. Without this release in the waking dream of utopian fancy the burdens of civilization would perhaps be unbearable. But if contemporary Fourierists evoke new states of consciousness (Charles Reich's Consciousness III is the most recent serial number), their derivative quality is patent, and they lack the freshness of new discovery. Why hearken to the gospels of the two Reichs, Marcuse, or Norman Brown when the grandest Pied Piper of them all lies open before you?

FRANK E. MANUEL

Washington Square, New York
January 1971

INTRODUCTION

MORE than one of our readers perhaps will be somewhat scandalised to see the name of Fourier enter into this collection,[1] following upon that of Adam Smith, of J. B. Say, of Ricardo:—but no one, surely, will be more surprised than Fourier himself would have been, had he been able to behold himself in such company. He professed, in fact, for all economists (whom, indeed, with the exception of J. B. Say, he appears not to have read), and for political economy itself, a supreme contempt, and he classed this science, along with metaphysics, moral philosophy, and politics, under the head of the "four uncertain sciences," an epithet which really implies nothing very dishonourable; but neither is it one altogether undeserved.

Everybody knows Fourier by name; nobody has read his books: consequently, although almost a contemporary, he already belongs to a legendary world. Cham's albums of caricature, which represent him with a tail having an eye at its extremity, Louis Reybaud's "Etudes sur les Réformateurs modernes," inspired by somewhat the same spirit, some words of his vocabulary, which by their oddity impressed themselves upon the mind—*phalanstère, papillonne, cabaliste, l'attraction passionelle*—: these are about the only records by which the public has been able to form an idea of Fourier, and this idea may be summed up in two words: he was a socialist of the worst type, that is, of the communist type, and a madman.

And I may add that those who perchance might have the courage to go back to Fourier's books themselves, would find themselves rather confirmed in their unflattering opinion, at least if they consulted the original editions, and if they stopped at a first examination. And indeed the sight of those enormous

[1] The Guillaumin, "Petite Bibliothèque Économique."—Tr.

volumes, without table of contents, without consecutive paging, that intentional absence of all plan (what he proudly termed "dispersed order"—"*l'ordre dispersé*"—and which it were more proper to term incoherent order), those headings of chapters or paragraphs which bear the titles of "*pivot direct*" or "*pivot inverse*," of "*cislégomène*," "*intermède*," and, quite at the end, of "*introduction*"; those pages where right in the midst of things the justification changes all of a sudden without our being able to discover why, and upon which it seems as though the printer had emptied all the letters of his case pell-mell; those X's and Y's which appear to dance a veritable saraband, now standing upright, now lying flat, now with heads drooped,—all this gives the impression of some conjuring book of a necromancer written in some very fabulous age.

It was not, therefore, a useless task to present to the public an abbreviated and, so to speak, a civilised edition (if I may be allowed to use an expression which our author would have found so distasteful!) of the works of Fourier. Either we are greatly deceived, or those who will read it will find a very different Fourier from the one they had represented to themselves. If they find a socialist,—and we shall take care not to rob him of this title : to do so would be to belittle him,—they will see at least that no one was more liberal than this socialist, and that his doctrines differed *toto orbe* from those of the communist school. If they find, besides, evidences of madness,—and neither would we wish to disguise this feature : to do that would be to disfigure him,—they will at least be able to assure themselves that it was an amiable madness, rubbing against wisdom at every step, abounding in keen and ingenious observations—which indeed is often the case with madmen ;—and, what is more surprising, they will find indicated a greater number of practical reforms which are capable of realisation,—some of them are indeed already realised,—than may be met with in the works of any socialist or even of any economist whatsoever.

I

CHARLES FOURIER [1] was born at Besançon, on the 7th of April, 1772 ; he died in Paris on the 7th of October, 1837. His whole biography might, if necessary, be condensed into these two lines ; it was not, in fact, distinguished by any memorable occurrence. Fourier did not instigate any conspiracies, like Gracchus Babœuf ; —he did not follow the advice of Saint Simon " to lead during the whole of the vigorous period of manhood the most original and active life possible," and did not, like him, lead the life of a *grand seigneur ;*—he had not, like Owen, the reputation of a great philanthropist, and did not, like him, give audience to princes and to emperors ;—he did not go to America to found a republic of Icaria like Cabet ;—he did not dazzle his contemporaries, like Lassalle, by an adventurous life and a romantic end ;—he was not even, like Karl Marx, the president of an International ;—no, he led the most prosaic life imaginable : that of a commercial traveller. Broker or clerk by turns in the cloth houses of Marseilles, Rouen, oftenest at Lyons, and, the last ten years of his life, at Paris, he terms himself a " shop-sergeant " (*sergent de boutique*) [2] and complains of not having had leisure for study. [3] And, indeed, when we consider that Fourier obtained all his intellectual and scientific education in reading-rooms which he

[1] In his first work, " Les Quatre Mouvements," Fourier wrote his name with two r's, but in all his other writings he adopted the orthography now known.

[2] " God has willed . . . that the ' Theory of Universal Movement ' (' Théorie du Mouvement Universel ') should fall to the share of an illiterate man (*sic*). It is a shop-sergeant who will confound those political and moral libraries, shameful fruit of ancient and modern charlatanry. Ah ! it is not the first time that God has made use of the humble to abase the proud, and that He has chosen the most obscure man to bring to the world the most important message."—" Quatre Mouvements," p. 151.

[3] " It is well to recall, now and then, that since the year 1799, when I discovered the germ of the calculus of Attraction, I have always been absorbed by my mercantile occupations, being hardly able to devote a few moments to passional problems (*problèmes passionels*), one of which often demands the continued research of several years. After passing my days in serving the knavery of merchants, and stupefying or brutalising myself by deceitful and degrading duties, I could not occupy the night in initiating myself in the true sciences."—" Manuscrits," 1851, p. 23.

visited in his spare moments, we cease to be astonished at the extravagance of his style or the fancifulness of his theories, and marvel rather at the abundance and, in general, the correctness of his classical citations, as well as at his intuition of the phenomena of Nature.

Fourier never married. He retained to the last all the habits and the passions of an old bachelor,—perhaps I should rather say, for his passions were very innocent ones, of an old maid. He was devoted to cats, flowers ; he appreciated good living ; he loved to follow regiments of soldiers through the streets, to keep time to the sound of military music ; he spent long hours watching the soldiers drill, not from any warlike taste, for no man had a more pacific nature, but from a love of uniforms, plumes, evolutions conducted scientifically. He was precise to excess in the arrangement of his life. " To-day, Candlemas, I have written twenty thirty-sixths of my book." Every day he came home upon the stroke of noon, because that was the hour he had set to meet capitalists who might be disposed to try his system,—and he awaited them punctually until his death. It has been said that he adored children. That is altogether inaccurate. He declares, on the contrary, upon every occasion, that they are insupportable creatures : his fastidious nature revolts against their noise, their disorder, their chattering. It is true that he allots them a very large place in his phalanstery, and that he even promises to nourish them on sweets, but then he really expects, by his system of education, to transform them into good children who will make no noise, be made to eat at a separate table, and be put to bed early.

If I insist upon facts of so intimate a nature, it is because they exercised a quite decisive influence upon Fourier's conception and upon the elaboration of his system. They alone can explain that passion for classing everything into phalanxes, series, groups ; the enormous place which the kitchen and the theatre occupy in his system ; that love of order, of symmetry, of labelling things ; that elaboration of the most insignificant details which give the world issuing from his brain the oldish, droll look of those little

Dresden or Chinese figures which we stand on our shelves. They alone can explain why the ideal of Fourier's dreams greatly resembles the life of a hotel and of a *table d'hôte*, and why the family, the home, paternal authority, always appeared to him like useless machinery, nuisances, which ought to be eliminated from the society of the future.

I should not forgive myself if I failed to add to this biographical sketch, brief as it is, two features. The first is that Fourier was, all his life,—not poverty-stricken, he was too regular in his mode of life to sink into distress, and he always kept his coat carefully brushed and wore a white necktie, but he was poor ; he earned from 1000 to 1500 francs a year, and he bore this poverty not only with dignity, but, what is better, with the most perfect serenity. The second is that, as far as may be judged by anecdotes related of him, he had in a high degree the spirit of charity, of true charity, that which hides itself.

Fourier, notwithstanding his preoccupation by his business duties, wrote an astonishing amount ; he wrote with the regularity of a writing machine, so many pages a day. In 1808, consequently at the age of thirty-six, he published his first work, " Théorie des Quatre Mouvements " ; in 1822, the most important of his works, " Traité de l'Association Domestique Agricole "; in 1829, the " Nouveau Monde Industriel," and finally in 1835 and 1836, that is, shortly before his death, " Fausse Industrie." But besides these four works, which represent about eight volumes, he left a vast quantity of manuscript, portions of which have been published since his death, some in a journal, the *Phalange*, and some in a separate volume. All these volumes bear, indeed, a strong resemblance to each other, especially as each contains the author's entire system, and exhibits, pell-mell, the same theories, reproduced, for the most part, in about the same terms ; whoever has read one of them, particularly the " Association Domestique Agricole," has read them all.

As we stated in the beginning, these books present themselves in a most extraordinary guise, such that it earned for its author the reputation of being a madman who ought to be confined.

There certainly is a good deal of the sensational,—of "puffing," as we should say to-day—in all this extravagance, but it is very difficult to discriminate in his case between what is unconscious and what is designed. I should not like to take an oath that he was not in real earnest when he declared : " I ALONE (*sic*) shall have confounded twenty centuries of political imbecility, and it is to me alone that present and future generations will owe the initiative of their boundless happiness. Before me, mankind lost several thousand years by fighting madly against Nature ; I am the first who has bowed before her, by studying attraction, the organ of her decrees ; she has deigned to smile upon the only mortal who has offered incense at her shrine ; she has delivered up all her treasures to me. Possessor of the book of Fate, I come to dissipate political and moral darkness, and, upon the ruins of the uncertain sciences, I erect the theory of universal harmony :

Exegi monumentum ære perennius." [1]

But it is difficult to believe that he is not in a manner making sport of the reader when he writes : " I shall defer until my third Memoir drawing the picture of combined order and the parallel between its delights and the afflictions of mind and body of the civilised. This parallel could not fail to excite the most unfortunate among them and drive them to despair, if it were not so circumspectly presented as to deaden its effect ; it is in order to accomplish this object that I shall purposely throw an air of coldness over my first Memoirs. . . ." [2]   We are unwilling to deprive ourselves of the pleasure of regarding this passage in a humorous light, in which aspect it is altogether charming.   And there are many others in the same tone.

The mad notions of Fourier—man's life prolonged to 144 years " on an average,"—the brine of the ocean transformed into a most agreeable acid taste—lions and sharks making way for " anti-lions " and " anti-sharks " of a very domestic nature—the Pole warmed and rendered fertile by a new aurora borealis, and

1 " Théorie des Quatre Mouvements," p. 285, *Epilogue.*
2 " Théorie des Quatre Mouvements," p. 95.

our planet enriched by four satellites, etc., etc.,—are well known ; but little else indeed is known of him.   There have even been lent to him—it is to the rich only that one lends—some that he never propounded, for instance the famous story of the tail with an eye at its extremity which the gravest economists continue to place upon his back, is a case in point, and a pure myth.[1]   We must observe, besides, that, as has been well remarked by M. Renouvier—the only philosopher who has deigned to accord this singular genius the attention he deserves[2]—this extravagance attaches principally to the minutiæ of the details, and to the preciseness of style whereby the author emphasises hypotheses which ought to be left in a certain vagueness.   If, for instance, he had confined himself to saying that one would in a single day be able to start from Marseilles, breakfast in Lyons, and dine in Paris, his prevision would have been considered most remarkable, but since he adds that the journey will be accomplished "upon the back of a supple and elastic porter which will be the anti-lion," we roar with laughter.   If he had said simply that people would some day be able to communicate instantaneously with each other from one end of the world to the other, it would have been regarded as a rare display of intellect ; but as he thought best to particularise by remarking : " A certain vessel leaving London arrives in China to-day ; to-morrow the planet Mars having been advised of the arrivals and movements of ships by the astronomers of Asia, will transmit the list to the astronomers of London," [3]—we shrug our shoulders and treat him as

[1] We are very glad to avail ourselves of the opportunity to explode this myth once for all, and that by the testimony of Fourier himself.   Fourier says that the inhabitants of the planets and the " *Solariens* " must be endowed with brilliant faculties denied to the " *Terriens*," and he adds : " I have remarked that this superiority is due principally to a member of which we are deprived, and which comprehends the following properties : protection in falling, powerful weapon, splendid ornament, gigantic strength, infinite dexterity, co-operation and support in all the bodily motions.   In discussing this problem, journalists devoid of imagination say that the *Solariens* resemble the demons of the farce of Saint Anthony, equipped with horns, prob osces, claws, and tails ; and that I wish to create men like this upon our globe ! "   This passage is found in the " Fausse Industrie," vol. ii., p. 5.

[2] See a series of articles upon the " Philosophy of Fourier," in the *Critique Philosophique* for the year 1883.

[3] " Unité universelle," vol. iii., p. 261.

an ignoramus.   If he had even confined himself to asserting in general terms that the planets exercise an influence upon the constitution and the evolution of animals and plants, one would not, perhaps, be so greatly astonished, but when he tells us that the planets Juno, Ceres, and Pallas each produce a species of gooseberry . . . ., that there ought to be a fourth and excellent kind of which we are deprived because the planet Phœbe (the moon), which would have generated it, is unfortunately dead,[1]— we cannot marvel sufficiently at an exhibition of such crack-brained folly! It is the form, then, that is more absurd than the substance.   And this absurdity is heightened by a peculiar language which Fourier concocted himself, a language picturesque at times, more often grotesque, and which does not even possess the advantage which big words often do, of imposing upon the public.

But if we do not allow ourselves to be repelled by these disagreeable appearances, and dive deeper into this medley, we soon find ourselves attracted by its singular charm.   This queer customer guides you with so sure a hand along the corridors of his phalanstery, he makes so many odd figures, whom he seems to know intimately, pass in review before you, he is so sure of his case, he makes every detail gleam with so many faces before your eyes, that in the end he hypnotises you, as a magnetiser does with the stopper of a carafe.   I do not believe that any man of this century has been gifted with greater imaginative power than this commercial clerk, save, perhaps, Edgar Poe.   That same precision of detail which produces so disastrous an effect when he rambles, throws his previsions, when they have a foundation, into startling relief.   When we read his pages,—some of which will be found in the present work,—upon the adulteration of merchandise, upon speculation and monopolies, the new industrial feudalism, the increase of intermediaries in petty commerce, the mobilisation of the soil, the necessity of international weights and measures, and of an international commercial language (a sort of Volapük), " the very certain and very general use of magnetism "

[1] This example is cited likewise by M. Renouvier, *op. cit.*

in the coming century, the development of the taste for and the cultivation of flowers, the protection due to animals, the possibility of modifying climatic conditions by appropriate vegetation, the approaching piercing of the Isthmus of Suez and the Isthmus of Panama " by canals through which the largest vessels will be able to pass," the organising of immense bodies of workmen—" industrial armies "—to carry out great public works in Africa and America,—when we read all this, we cannot conceive that these pages were written as much as three-quarters of a century ago. We have here a veritable genius for divining, something resembling that gift of second-sight, which, indeed, if one put any faith in popular superstition, is the privilege of the simple-minded.

II

IT is not easy to give a general view of the system of Fourier, for it is above all noticeable for its exuberance of details and the precision with which each one is analysed. We shall, however, try to bring out its large lines.

Fourier starts out with the *à priori* idea that there must be a plan of God, that is to say, a certain social order conformable to God's will, and such as may secure the perfect happiness of all mankind. The whole thing is to discover this plan : the entire social problem reduces itself to a sort of divining-rod task. Fourier feels sure that he has discovered the secret. Assuming as a postulate the pre-established correspondence between the planetary and the social world, he asserts that the mechanism which causes both to move must be the same, namely : attraction. To Newton, to whom he constantly compares himself, the glory of having revealed this principle and expounded its laws as regards the material world ; to him, Fourier, the honour of having revealed it and expounded its laws as regards the moral world.[1]   And how

[1] The manner in which Fourier himself relates the history of his discovery (whose date he fixes, with his habitual precision, at the year 1798), is sufficiently amusing :—" Chance counts for half in the success of a man of genius. . . . I myself paid tribute to it when I discovered the calculus of attraction.

may the existence of attraction in human beings be recognised? It is revealed in the simplest manner by the existence of the passions, that is, of those vivid and spontaneous forces which impel man towards a desired object. Hence Fourier designates the mainspring of action, according to him, of human society, by the term " passional attraction " (" *attraction passionelle* ").

If the existing order of things, which is designated by the name of civilisation, is in reality so miserable and confused, it is because legislators, imbued with the principles of a false morality, have taxed their ingenuity to obstruct the scope of human passions, and have thus caused them to be diverted from their true object. We must, on the contrary, find a combination where the passions of man, all without exception,—even those which we wrongly term bad, since they, like the others, have been given him by God,—may act normally, and we shall then see the free play of the passions producing universal harmony.

In other words, up to the present day, the effort to change man so as to adapt him to his environment has been persistently pursued : we must follow the opposite scent and change the environment so as to adapt it to man. In reality the environment may much more readily be modified than man, for the former is the work of man while the latter is the work of God.

This new environment is to be produced by association, not, however, by any sort of association, but by a particular one, very profound and very complex, that one only, as we might imagine,

. . . An apple was for me, as for Newton, a guiding compass. For this apple, which is worthy of fame, a traveller who dined with me at Février's restaurant in Paris paid the sum of fourteen sous. I had just come from a district where the same kind of apples, and even superior ones, sold for a half-liard, that is to say, more than a hundred for fourteen sous. I was so struck by this difference of price between places having the same temperature, that I began to suspect there must be something radically wrong in the industrial mechanism, and hence originated the researches, which, after four years, caused me to discover the theory of series of industrial groups, and, consequently, the laws of universal motion missed by Newton. . . .

" I have since then noticed that we can reckon four apples as celebrated, two for the disasters which they caused, Adam's apple and that of Paris, and two for the services they rendered to science, Newton's apple and mine. Does not this quadrille of apples deserve a page of history? "—" Manuscrits," year 1851, p. 17.

which Fourier discovered and of which he has expounded the mechanism. It must be observed, indeed, that Fourier nowise thinks that this combination is capable of being produced in virtue of a spontaneous and necessary evolution, but that it was necessary to discover and apply it. Our author thinks, however, that it could have been discovered very much earlier. Already before the Christian era, in the time of the republics of Greece, it could have been done. The time was ripe for it. Mankind has lost two thousand years, solely on account of the rhetoricians and moralists.

Let us show by some examples how Fourier expects to go about organising his industrial world solely upon the principle of attraction. It does not seem that man is naturally drawn to labour. Yet labour is absolutely indispensable to the economic life of society. How emerge from this dilemma? If, in civilised society, replies Fourier, labour is repulsive, it is because it is so falsely organised that it does not respond to any of man's instincts; and Fourier enumerates, with very remarkable critical acumen by the way, all the causes which render labour repulsive in our "civilised" society (we must lay stress on the word civilised, because for the Indian the chase, for the nomad the raising of cattle, does not lack attraction); we shall not enumerate them here; the reader will find them in the extracts; besides, one may foretell what they are. Labour, then, must be so organised that it should be attractive, that is to say, that man should take to it from inclination, from passion, and we must, therefore, determine by analysis what are the motor passions of man which must be brought into play in this instance. Fourier finds three such passions: the *papillonne*, which is the need of change and variety;—the *cabaliste*, which is the love of intrigue, and that emulation which results in rivalry;—the *composite*, which seeks satisfaction in a compound pleasure affecting at once the mind and the body. Let us, therefore, organise branches of labour of a pleasant character, such as the cultivation of flowers or fruits, which are of a nature to give rise at the same time to enjoyments, —sensuous, esthetic, and moral,—let us organise them simultaneously and in the same place, so that the labourers may easily go from one to the other.—Let us group the labourers in such a manner as to unite those having the same tastes, and let us, at the same time, oppose these groups to each other, in order to develop their *esprit de corps* and to keep them on the alert by a ceaseless rivalry ; and when all the passional springs of action (*resorts passionnels*) shall thus have been brought into play by that mechanism, of which we have given but a very imperfect idea, but which is in reality extraordinarily complicated, we shall see men rush to their work, just as, on a field of battle, where, likewise, the "passionate springs" are brought into play, we see them rush to their death.

Another example. Self-interest, that interest which in every distribution impels us to claim the larger share, seems but little compatible with the maintenance of harmony, and yet it cannot be eliminated, since it is the mainspring of production. Here again Fourier asserts that the problem may be solved by bringing into play certain passional springs of action. He divides the total product (following a proportion more or less arbitrary, but which is of little moment in this explanation) between three factors : Labour, Capital, and Talent,—and he organises things in such a way that there is no one in the association who does not figure in at least the first two designations, and who does not hope to figure in the third ; hence it is not to the interest of anyone to contest the share assigned to each of these three factors, the general prosperity of the association being, moreover, dependent upon satisfying each of them. This is not all ; this first general division having been effected, a sub-division is made by series and groups, each series receiving a share more or less considerable, according as the kind of work to which it devotes itself is more or less attractive or more or less useful to society. Here again, as each labourer figures in a great number of series, by reason of the various occupations in which he is to engage, it will be to no one's interest that one series should be favoured to the detriment of another. Without pursuing the exposition of this system into its ultimate ramifications, what I have just said will suffice to give an idea of the plan of Fourier, which consists in such an intimate blending, in the mechanism of distribution, of personal interest and collective interest, that any conflict between them shall become impossible.

Fourier, analysing by turns what in civilised society are called " the vices," endeavours to demonstrate how, under the *régime* of association they would all become sources of harmony ; for example, inconstancy in love (and upon this theme he indulges in variations which have proved somewhat embarrassing even to his disciples), the love of luxury, gluttony, the love of disorder and dirt in children. As regards gluttony, for instance, he show that under an industrial *régime* in which the cultivation of fruits and vegetables of superior kinds and great variety will be the chief branch of industry, the education and refinement of taste of the consumers will become a necessity. He explains that if children prefer sweetmeats to dry bread for their lunch, this proves that Providence, in giving them that instinct, knew very well what it was doing ; it foresaw the day when agriculture would be superseded by arboriculture, and the production of insipid grain by that of savoury fruits, and with this in view it had instilled in advance these natural instincts into man ; it is not the fault of Providence if we have totally failed to comprehend its intentions or intimations . . ., and the author continues thus to an unconscionable length, with a mixture of extravagance and madness which is highly diverting, and which makes us think of the harangues that Don Quixote in the Sierra Morena delivered to the astonished goatherds.

Since the new social order is to be based solely upon attraction, it goes without saying that Fourier has no thought of employing force. Never, in fact, does he appeal to legislators, to government, to an authority, to a coercive power of any sort ;[1] I do not

[1] Impartiality compels me to say, however, that in an inconspicuous corner of his works I have found an appeal to the intervention of the legislator. " Is it indeed by freedom that the civilised man can be led to wisdom ? No : he must be forced. When the adoption of large fellies was made compulsory, all the drivers raised a loud outcry, and two years afterwards these same men were desirous of the change. . . . What has not been done after the same fashion in regard to the metric system ? . . . . Such is the civilised man, a

even know whether the word State which to-day serves to characterise all more or less socialist schools, appears a single time in his books. In this he belongs wholly to the most uncompromising liberal school:—and since he does not even recognise the necessity of the police State, one might go so far as to say that he belongs to the anarchist school, if that term did not clash so strangely with his love of order and of symmetry. It is upon free individual initiative alone that he reckons to make a trial of his system,—an initiative which he solicits, begs for, addressing himself to the great capitalists and to disengaged princes with a touching pertinacity,—and it is solely upon the contagion of example that he relies to propagate his system throughout the world. As regards ways and means, he gives proof of an irreproachable orthodoxy: he has no thought of proceeding by any way but that of social experiment.

Since the new order is based upon attraction, it also goes without saying that Fourier does not think of having recourse to revolution. He has a horror of revolutionary methods, from which, indeed, he himself had been a personal sufferer, for he had been imprisoned at Lyons, and had almost felt the cold touch of the guillotine at his throat. Not only is he not a revolutionist, but he is not even a republican: he organises a sort of feudal hierarchy which ascends by degrees from the unarch or baron to the omniarch or emperor: he even holds in reserve a number of thrones for his new *régime*, some of them elective, it is true, but others hereditary, which he offers with a lordly grace to all kings in exile, to all disengaged princes who might desire them. To speak the truth, monarchy, in his system, reduces itself to a purely decorative form: it is there *ad pompam*

being without reason: it is necessary for his own good to use coercive measures with him. . . . Will they take offence at this avowal? Let them refute me by facts, by taking the initiative in real liberty, in association." (" Unité universelle," vol. iii., p. 146, Note.) But we should be wrong in regarding this stray passage, embodied in a note, and which is evidently nothing but an outburst of ill-humour, and in direct opposition to his entire scheme, as a real expression of his thought.

This is found much more faithfully and strongly expressed in that other phrase of his *à propos* of the Jesuits of Paraguay: " All that is founded upon force is fragile and denotes the absence of genius."

ed ostentationem, as lawyers express it in Latin,—useless, in fact, since attraction will suffice to keep the world going. Neither is he anti-clerical in the sense in which that word is understood to-day. Not only does he promise "not to worry either ministers or priests," but, further, to secure them a considerable place in the new order. He even declares religions to be "far superior to the uncertain sciences," because "they have had the honour of passing true judgments upon the condition of civilised man : they rightly consider him in a state of exile and of divine punishment." ("Manuscrits," vol. 1853-1856, p. 293.)

It is not only in the domain of politics and religion, but also in that of political economy that, no matter what one may think, Fourier shows himself resolutely conservative. He purposes to maintain property, heredity, interest on capital, and, above all, the inequality between the rich and the poor, which "enters into God's plan," and which, consequently, enters also into his, and to such a degree that he declares in advance any associative [1] experiment as sterile and useless, in which people of very unequal fortunes shall not have been brought to take part. It is noticeable, moreover, that Fourier nearly always addresses himself by preference to the wealthy class rather than to what is at the present day termed the working-class : he assures the rich that he desires to make them still richer, and it is by the allurement of enormous dividends, which rise to eighteen or thirty-six per cent., —precisely as in the prospectuses of an issue of stock,—it is even by the far more extraordinary prospect of numerous bequests to be received by them from their fellow-associates that he seeks to entice them. Regarded on this side, Fourier's system may be characterised as thoroughly "*bourgeois.*" He shrugs his shoulders at the communistic theories of Owen or even at the mitigated communism of Saint-Simon. [2]

[1] Associative = *societaire.* *See* note, p. 53.—Tr.
[2] " I attended the service of the Simonians last Sunday. One cannot conceive how these sacerdotal play-actors can command so large a following. Their dogmas are not admissible ; they are monstrosities at which we must shrug our shoulders ; to preach, in the nineteenth century, the abolition of property and heredity !"—Letter of the 28th of January, 1831 (quoted by Pellarin, " Vie de Fourier ").

But the phalanstery, it will be asked. The phalanstery, the characteristics of which have been totally misconceived, in nowise resembles the communistic establishments, for instance, founded in America by the disciples of Cabet or of Mother Anne. There is nothing either of the barracks or of the convent about it : the inmates do not sleep in dormitories and they do not mess together. We must picture it to ourselves like one of those great hotels of Switzerland or of the United States,—frequently established upon shares,—where are found combined nearly all the comforts of life : there are common rooms for eating, conversation, or reading, but each one may be served at a separate table or even in his own rooms. In the phalanstery also, apartments are to be had at all prices, and *tables d'hôte* of three different classes, without reckoning the children's table and that for invalids, and service by order, otherwise termed *à la carte*, for those who prefer it.

To this great *hotel-pension* there is attached, it is true, an agricultural and in part industrial enterprise (*exploitation*) which is likewise collective, but which is neither more nor less so than undertakings founded upon shares. Everyone receives in shares the exact amount of the capital he was able to put into the association on entering it, or of the savings he has by degrees been able to accumulate while belonging to it. Individual property, it is true, is bound to be gradually transformed completely into common sharehold property,—but that is an evolution quite conformable with the views of the most orthodox political economy, and which M. de Molinari, for instance, predicts for us with no less assurance than Fourier.[1] And Fourier hopes by this mobilisation of property to succeed in making everybody a co-proprietor, so that the poorest ones in Harmony might be able to say on seeing the phalanstery : "My palace, my lands, my houses." In the distribution of the total product of the enter-

[1] "The innumerable multitude of enterprises, agricultural, industrial, commercial, etc., will be owned by groups of shareholders and bondholders, in whose ranks will be found associated men of all stations, of all nationalities, of all colours."—De Molinari, "L'évolution economique du dix-neuvième siècle," p. 437.

prise, he allots only five-twelfths to labour, four-twelfths to capital, and three-twelfths to talent [1] : now this is a proportion in which it cannot be said that labour has the lion's share, for it is quite certain that even under the present order of things, the portion of this factor of production amounts to not less than five-twelfths, since, according to the calculation of the collectivists themselves, it is slightly more. And surely capital would declare itself very well satisfied with the portion guaranteed it by Fourier, for it is doubtful whether it to-day carries off more than a third of the total production. All this, then, is of a nature to reassure the most circumspect.

However, after having thus rehabilitated him with the economists, I should not wish to discredit him entirely with the socialists, or make him appear too much of a mere *bonhomme*. These, then, are the main points of the system in which the socialist spirit manifests itself :

1° The interest or dividend allowed the shares is not the same for them all : they are divided into three classes : those whose rate of interest is enormous, something like 36 to 40 per cent. ; others, where it is less ; the last, finally, where it is very small, that is to say, about equal to our usual rate of 5 or 6 per cent. (which under the associative *régime*, where production will be superabundant, will be considered very low). Now the shares in the first category (*actions ouvrières*) will not be assigned except to those who have a very small number of them, one or at most two ; having received this allotment, they will not be able to own any shares but those in the second category (*actions foncières*), and even these in rather limited quantity : if they should wish to go beyond this limit they will only have a right to the third category (*actions banquières*). The object of this mechanism, which is childish enough, is that, contrary to the present order of things, small amounts of capital shall bring in much better returns than large ones, and that it shall be much easier for the poor to start a fortune than for the rich to augment theirs.

[1] Or again : six-twelfths to labour, four-twelfths to capital, and two-twelfths to talent, a proportion which also would quite well suit Fourier, for, says he, " the sum of the two extremes would equal double the mean, $2+6=2\times4$ " !

2° A minimum as regards food, lodging, clothing, and even amusements,—a minimum, modest but "very decent,"—will be guaranteed to all the members of the association, that is to say,— supposing Fourier's system to be made universal, as it is meant to be,—to all men. This is one of the most important features of Fourier's programme. It does not at first sight seem that there is anything more in it than a system of compulsory legal assistance on a great scale. But what is weighty about it is that Fourier allows this minimum *without conditions*, that is to say, without demanding that he who profits by it shall furnish a certain amount of work or give proof of his inability to work. The objection which strikes one at first blush, namely, that under these conditions nobody would take the trouble to work, does not concern Fourier. He recognises that in the state of civilisation the objection is an insurmountable one, because there man works only to gain his bread,—but under the associative *régime*, in which man works for pleasure and from "passion," the knowledge that his place at the dinner-table is assured will not stop him : quite the contrary. And Fourier adds, and his remark is a very just one, that the guarantee of this minimum is the condition *sine quâ non* of the existence of his phalanstery, that is to say, of the life in common between persons belonging to all classes of society : it alone can allow the poor to live in harmony with the rich, and without envy ;—it alone, too, can allow the rich to find pleasure in the society of the poor, by rendering them men "of good company," and maintaining them at a certain moral and intellectual level.

3° The wage system will be abolished, labour being thenceforth renumerated solely by a share in the profits (the five-twelfths). The wage system is, in fact, incompatible with the dominant idea of Fourier's system, that of attractive labour ; mercenary labour cannot be attractive any more than forced labour, and precisely because it is in part forced. It is especially the wage system as applied to domestic service that is repellent to Fourier, and the way in which he proposes to abolish it is one of the most original and most touching parts of his books. As for the wages of industrial labour, the solution indicated by Fourier as early as the beginning of this century is no other than that which has been applied with so much success in the Swiss *Familistère*, the Leclaire establishment, the *Bon Marché;* that is to say, profit-sharing, carrying the workmen, little by little, to a co-proprietorship in the business. We see, then, that in this solution there is nothing revolutionary.

If we pass now to what I shall term his economic programme, I shall sum it up under the following eight heads :

1° *To aim at reform in the method of production rather than the method of distribution.*—The social question, for him, does not lie in the inequality of wealth but in its insufficiency. For him, the existing organisation involves a frightful waste of the productive forces, which is the cause of there not being sufficient wealth for the poor nor even for the rich who falsely fancy themselves rich, while they are merely a little less miserable than the poor. It is in the organism of production, then, that lies the evil which we must cure.

2° *To lay stress upon agricultural production rather than upon industrial production.*—Industrial production does not enter into God's plans ; or, if one prefers, man is not naturally attracted to industrial labour, save to some certain kinds on a small scale. But the work done in factories, the labour of extracting the products of mines, which is necessarily allied with that work, are employments repellent to man, and are, besides, in great part needless. In reality, good quality, which ensures the durability of products, the economy resulting from a life in common, the simplicity of manners which will do away with fashion and its ruinous caprices, will allow the consumption of industrial products to be reduced to a minimum. It is the consumption of alimentary products which cannot be reduced, but should, on the contrary, be enormously increased. Agricultural production must, therefore, be the pivot of all production, as it is also the natural vocation of man. It is that, too, which in the world of Harmony is destined to fill the whole scene. Fourier reserves for industrial work only a quarter of the time at disposal, and that only for such work as may be considered the accessory of agricultural labour,—weaving, spinning, and the arts of the carpenter, locksmith, basket-maker, etc.

3° *To transform agricultural industry by devoting it exclusively to horticulture and arboriculture.*—Agricultural labour, it may be objected to Fourier, is not necessarily more attractive than industrial labour; to till the earth has always been regarded, on the contrary, as the type of painful toil, of toil which is done "with the sweat of one's brow." Assuredly, replies Fourier. And by agricultural production we do not mean what has been almost exclusively designated by that name since Triptolemus, that is to say, the cultivation of wheat. This voracious grain requires for its cultivation relatively enormous areas; it hardly produces euough, upon a given area, to nourish a small number of people; it imposes, for its cultivation, as well as for its transformation into bread, the severest labour under which mankind has ever been made to groan,—that of the plough, the millstone, the kneading-trough; and, finally, it furnishes but an insipid aliment, good at most only "for the civilised." It is from the cultivation of fruits and vegetables, the raising of fowls and bees, from fish-culture, that we must henceforth demand the nourishment of mankind. It is these products alone that will permit us to obtain from a relatively small area a food supply at once abundant, varied, savoury, and constantly renewed; they alone brighten the earth by making its surface a garden, the garden of Eden; they alone, above all, answer the natural tastes of man and turn labour into a pleasure. As one of his disciples says, "The young wife waters her flowers, the old soldier lays out the borders of his little garden, and the student grafts his trees; the banker designs tortuous paths in his English garden; the simple citizen tries to lose himself among the windings of his microscopic parterre; the grisette decorates her window with a curtain of climbing-plants." [1]

4° *Not to employ any other method of production than production on a great scale.*—Upon this point, Fourier being in accord with

[1] Renaud, "De la Solitarité," p. 67.

all economists and even all socialists, it is useless to insist, unless to call attention to the fact that production on a great scale, now become so common, was not so much so at the time when Fourier proclaimed it.—It is for the purpose of carrying on production on a great scale that he had conceived the Phalanx, an association of about 1800 persons working a piece of land a square league in extent, say about 5000 acres ; that is an area which will appear considerable if we reflect that in Fourier's system the work is to consist chiefly of market-gardening.—It is for great undertakings which would require the activity of larger masses, that he proposes to have recourse to the industrial armies.

5° *To carry the division of labour to its ultimate limits.*—It is a trite maxim of political economy since Adam Smith that agricultural production does not lend itself to division of labour, and this proposition seems to have a basis so far as regards the raising of annuals, such as we cultivate, but it ceases to be true for the growing of market-garden and horticultural products. Here, on the contrary, it is readily understood that each producer should make a speciality of a certain variety of flowers, or fruits, or vegetables. Fourier, therefore, proposes to divide his phalanx into 135 series,—growers of cabbage, radishes, cherries, etc., and to subdivide these themselves into as many groups and sub-groups as there are varieties in each species.

6° *In order to correct the monotony of specialisation carried to an extreme, to have recourse to variety and the alternation of labour.*— This is, of his entire scheme, the point to which he attaches the most importance. He points out, surely not without reason, that, in order that specialisation should produce all the good results which may be expected from it, it is by no means indispensable that this specialisation should be limited to a single object. A man may very well be trained as a specialist in several different branches, and nevertheless bring to bear upon each the maximum ability and dexterity of which he is capable. And in going by turn from one task to another he will have the advantage of escaping the stupefying effect of monotony, and of satisfying that need of change, that "*papillone*," which according to Fourier, as we know, constitutes one of the fundamental passions of man.

7° *To employ in consumption the system of association on a great scale, in order to avoid the waste inherent in housekeeping.*— Consumption on a great scale ("*la grande consommation*") appears to Fourier an indispensable corollary to production on a great scale ("*la grande production*") and for the same economic reasons. The calculation of the enormous saving which must result from this consumption in common, is one of the favourite themes of Fourier. His methodical cast of mind delights in these household accounts.

8° *To accomplish the suppression of all intermediaries by constituting great autonomous associations which shall be self-sufficient or shall procure by direct exchange with similar associations the products they need.*—These autonomous associations are, naturally, the phalansteries : however, as a preparatory measure, Fourier recommended the institution of communal warehouses designed to receive in storage and to sell directly to the consumers agricultural products, and to buy directly from the producers raw materials, implements, and all the articles of consumption needed by their members.

III

SUCH, in its large outlines, is the system of Fourier. Contrary to general belief, its character is not essentially socialistic, but if we compare it with those of the great economic schools, we find that it presents notable points of contact with each of them, as well as essential differences.

With the liberal school it has in common its absolute confidence in the liberty of the individual and its antipathy to all coercive intervention :—but it differs from it in that it declares that before inaugurating the rule of *laisser faire* and *laisser passer* we must first place man in an environment prepared *ad hoc*, civilised environment rendering the normal development of mankind an absolute impossibility.

With the optimist school of Bastiat, which, in this point, it anticipated by thirty years, it has in common its firm assurance that universal harmony must be the spontaneous outcome of the free play of individual interests, and that the social order ought not to be less perfect than the order which reigns in the planetary system :—but it differs from it in that, instead of believing this harmony already realised in the existing order of things, he considers, on the contrary, this order of things anarchical and barbarous, and looks forward to a new heaven and a new earth.

With the Christian school it has in common its faith in the existence of a foreordained providential plan from which man wandered and which it is now our concern to recover, if we desire the reign of peace : but it differs from it radically by its belief in the innate goodness of man, by its theory that all the passions of man lead him naturally towards good and that he could not do better than to yield to them, finally by its negation of moral law, of duty, of sin.

With the socialist school, in conclusion, it has in common the vehemence of its attacks upon competition, commerce, domestic life, upon civilisation in general, as well as its tendency to see everything painted in bright colours in the society of the future ; it has in common also the guarantee of a minimum and the abolition of the wage system ; but it differs from it radically by its respect for the wealthy classes, for property, inheritance, capital, and all that is commonly spoken of as constituting the foundations of social order.

One cannot, then, deny to the system of Fourier the merit of originality. As to its shortcomings and its errors, they are no less evident.

His method is, to begin with, *à priori* to a degree that passes all bounds. I know very well that Fourier denies it, and declares that we must "observe the things we wish to know and not imagine them" [1] ; but when he proceeds to explain in minute

---

[1] Here, by way of a curiosity, are the rules of method laid down by Fourier :
To trace ideas to their origin.
Not to believe Nature limited to known methods.

detail what God's plan was in regard to us, and not only in regard to our poor little earth, but all the other planets, just as if he had been present and taken part in the celestial councils —it is hard to think that he has remained faithful to his maxim. By this we do not mean that correct, even penetrating observations are lacking in the works of Fourier—they contain gems of that kind,—but for this strange observer the facts observed, instead of being the rock upon which to build his system, serve but as a springing-board on which, every time, he gets a new start to rebound to the very stars !

To take as a starting-point that God "who is a skilful mechanician " must have employed the same force in the material as in the moral world, that is, attraction,—to infer, like Pythagoras or like Bastiat, from the harmony which reigns in the movements of the planets a like harmony in the relation of human beings,—all this is philosophy of a childish enough sort. We do not at all know whether the sidereal world is perfect, or even whether there is a single planet besides our own where life may find the conditions necessary for its development, and even admitting that it did, that would offer but small ground upon which to base conclusions regarding social relations.

To reckon in man twelve fundamental passions belongs to an evidently fantastic or rather mystic psychology,—the number 12 having been evidently chosen only because it made a better working number than 11 or 13. Doubtless in certain respects this analysis may be considered superior to that of the classical school which recognises only a single motive in man, that of self-interest, and regards all the other sentiments as simply disturbing elements, or negligible quantities which ought to be left out of account. The passional system of Fourier offers a richer

To explore in its entirety the domain of Nature.
To simplify the motive power in every mechanism.
To observe the things we wish to know and not imagine them.
To doubt and consult experience.
To go from the known to the unknown by analogy.
To proceed by analysis and synthesis.
To believe that everything is connected, unitary, in the system of the universe.—(U. U., i., 197.)

key-board and one probably in closer conformity with reality than the hedonistic principle which serves as a basis for all the deductions of pure political economy, but he takes great care to suppress in this key-board all the keys which might disturb the final harmony. For instance, among the passions of man, Fourier completely ignores the existence of indolence, envy, and jealousy,—to mention only these. Now even admitting that the first two might be considered as springing simply from our state of civilisation, and, consequently, susceptible of disappearing with it,—one cannot, at all events, say as much of jealousy, which certainly is as natural as the instinct of reproduction itself, with which, for the rest, it seems allied among brutes as well as in man.

Attractive labour is itself a purely *à priori* conception. It is with reason that Fourier regarded this as the pivot of his system,—for it is quite certain that if labour were a pleasure instead of a pain, all economic phenomena without exception would be different from what they are,—but observation does not offer to our view attractive labour anywhere. It is true that Montesquieu found it possible to say : " There is no climate on earth where free men could not be induced to work. Because the laws were bad, people were found to be lazy ; because they were lazy, they were put in slavery," [1] but he meant to say by that not that labour was not a pain, but that it was a pain which man accepted courageously if it had as correctives liberty and property. Doubtless, also, it is true that man finds delight and his true destiny in the exercise of a certain physical and intellectual activity,—that absolute inaction, for instance that of a prisoner under a rule of complete isolation in a cell, is a torment more cruel than the eternal task of Sisyphus in the infernal regions—but this activity is enjoyable, properly speaking, only when it finds its satisfaction, its proper end, in itself; as soon as it is only a means to gain an end determined in advance, only a condition to an ulterior enjoyment, then it requires painful effort, and can cause only such pleasure as arises from the satisfaction of duty accomplished ;—and that is exactly why

[1] " Esprit des Lois," book xv., chap. viii.

certain exercises (such as walking, rowing, dancing) may be, just according to the end in view, but without changing their nature, either painful labour or amusing sport. It is not difficult to turn any labour into play, but at the same time it becomes sterile. I have no doubt that the labours of which Fourier makes us spectators in his phalanstery, such as cultivating roses or gathering cherries in joyous company, may indeed be very attractive, and we should, doubtless, take extreme pleasure in them, but I doubt greatly that labour conducted in such a manner would prove productive. The noblest employments, the most attractive it would seem, that of the artist and the poet, even they, in order to become productive, impose the strain and anguish of travail. Manual labour forms no exception. Take even the kind of labour to which Fourier was so partial, and to which he hopes to bring back by degrees all human industry—gardening ; it may, no doubt, be charming for one who demands nothing but the pleasure itself of gardening, but if she has to supply the markets with provisions for a great city, it becomes more arduous perhaps than any other. A monograph on the market gardeners of the outskirts of Paris[1] depicts them to us ; " beginning their work before dawn, spending the day gathering vegetables, cleaning them, arranging them in baskets, loading the waggons, no matter what the weather ; and on days preceding market-day, prolonging their labour to ten o'clock at night, then throwing themselves upon their beds, and after a few hours' repose, rising, mounting the waggon, and starting in rain or frost so as to reach the market-place about four o'clock in the morning." The Chinese, too, have transformed agriculture into a sort of market-garden culture which is wonderfully productive, but at what cost ? by transporting upon their shoulders in order to scatter over the soil " human manure " . . ., might this perchance be one of the forms of attractive labour ?

Neither does his organisation of property appear to be based upon a just analysis of the desires and the needs of human nature. We must observe that,—contrary to the collectivists, who abolish individual property in the instruments of production (land and

[1] " Maraîchers de Deuil," par Urbain Guérin, " Ouvriers des deux mondes."

capital), and retain it as to articles of consumption,—Fourier retains property (mobilised, it is true, under the form of shares) in land and capital, but desires, it seems, to abolish it as to articles of consumption by his system of hotel life. Now, if it were necessary to choose between these two forms of maiming the right of property, I should prefer that of the collectivists : this would not touch, like that of Fourier, the most intimate and most sensitive fibres of our being. For, if it is desirable, from the point of view of individual development, that everyone shall have the possibility of being an owner of lands or houses, of registered bonds, or bonds payable to bearer, at least it cannot be said that this is indispensable to happiness,—there are plenty of people who do not enjoy that satisfaction, and who regard themselves as happy in spite of it ;—but it may on the other hand be maintained that what is indispensable to the happiness of private life is the ability to own the things which surround us, which we touch, and into which we put our memories and a part of ourselves.

Finally, without pursuing these criticisms further, we may indulge in the regret that Fourier, in the perspectives which he unrolls before our eyes, believed it necessary to tempt men by allurements relatively gross. Those dividends of thirty and thirty-six per cent., that quadruple and sextuple product, that land yielding henceforth two harvests a year, all this resembles a little too closely the prospectuses of those suspicious companies which we see spring up on the eve of financial crashes. That country in which people will partake of five meals a day, and where they will eat sweetmeats instead of bread, is simply the land of the foolish tales we listened to in our childhood : it was called the country where things could be had for the asking. The new world that Fourier pictures to his disciples resembles a little too closely the paradise which Mahomet promised his followers,—even the houris are not wanting ! All this is a low enough moral conception. We do not know what the society of the future will be, but what we do know is that that society, whatever it may be, will be superior to our own only in so far as it shall have succeeded in elevating the thoughts and desires of man, and that this will not be attained by treading a path of roses. That continual effort of man to reach a goal which he will never attain, that struggle against himself which constitutes his wretchedness and his dignity—of all this tragic side of human destiny Fourier had not even a suspicion,[1] and he does not, therefore, deserve to take rank among the great reformers.

But thus much granted to criticism, there is still much to be gleaned from the work of Fourier : it abounds in suggestive views, and here and there, through the clouds, in luminous and astonishingly profound vistas of the future. No book—since that of the Sibyls—has contained more oracles, and if among the number there are some that are of but little more value than those of Delphi, there are others which will very probably be realised, which are already on the road to realisation, and thereby justify what we have called the divining genius of Fourier.

Is not, for instance, the preponderance of industrial over agricultural production a deplorable side of our economic organisation, and have we not here a displacement of equilibrium contrary to the nature of things, and growing more and more menacing ? That evil which tends to become chronic, and which we designate by the term industrial crises, is it aught else at bottom but a disproportion more and more marked between the production of necessary wealth, that is, alimentary commodities, and that of relatively superfluous wealth, that is, industrial products,— a disproportion which is evidenced by a disastrous rise in the price of the first, and a fall, unavailing enough, in the price of the second ? Is it not a pity to see our time reserve all its inventions, its most powerful machines, the resources of steam and electricity, for the production of pins and envelopes, when the production of

[1] The man who was considered the most eminent disciple of Fourier, and the only one who has realised a part of his scheme, expressed himself thus regarding his master : "The doctrine wherein he maintains that every man, whatever his character, is a harmonious being, appears to me a preconceived idea. This fundamental error is based upon the idea that man is such as God has made him, instead of a progressive being whose duty it is to labour for his own perfection, and who is what he makes himself."—Letter of the 18th of April, reproduced in the " Bulletin du Mouvement social," 1884.

grain and meat is, according to the avowal of all agriculturists, so deplorably behindhand ? Is this, then, the future reserved to our race, to crowd more and more into cities black with smoke and tainted with wretchedness, and do not several of the great economic schools to-day take as their watchword the same great cry which urged Fourier on at the beginning of this century : Return to the soil !

The transformation of agriculture into horticulture, again, is that indeed such a puerile conception ? Does not agricultural evolution tend, in fact, under the pressure of a constantly growing population, to become more and more intensive, and is not market-gardening the last step in intensive cultivation ? Are not already the suburbs of the great centres of population devoted entirely to market-gardening ? And what will the whole of Europe be some years hence if not one gigantic suburb stretching without a break from one capital to another ? Europe will then abandon the cultivation of cereals and the raising of cattle with-out regret, first, because it will no longer have large enough tracts of land at its disposal for these purposes, and further, because America, Africa, and Asia will engage in them in its stead, and at a less cost ; and it will no longer persist in a defensive war of tariffs, as futile as it is onerous. It is related of Mr. Gladstone that, some English proprietors having come to him to complain of the competition of American wheat, he replied to them : " Cultivate roses ! The Americans will not send you roses." Charming and profound remark ! which is, however, only a picturesque expression of the system of Fourier. Yes, our grand-sons will cultivate roses,—why not ? if we may trust Candide, the last word of philosophy is to cultivate one's garden ; why should it not also be the last word of political economy ?

Upon the advantages of production on a great scale, of the division of labour, upon the abuses of the multiplicity of inter-mediaries, and the adulteration of commodities, there is no need of justifying Fourier : his case is won in advance. We may, however, on this last point, permit ourselves to call attention to the fact that not only did Fourier denounce the evil with a caustic

energy and a precision which have left but little to be said after
him, but that, furthermore, he pointed out exactly the true
remedy ; one which is only to-day beginning to be applied on a
great scale,—I refer to the agricultural syndicates and the
co-operative associations of consumers. As will be seen in the
ensuing extracts, he described most accurately the characteristics
of these associations and delineated their *rôle* and functions with
the greatest exactitude half a century in advance, by exhibiting
the mechanism of his *"comptoirs communaux"* ; and the influence
exercised by Fourier upon the development of co-operation,
particularly in America, is certainly not less than that attributed
to Owen.

As regards what is usually spoken of as the social question, or
the wages-problem, has anyone up to the present day shown us a
more practical solution,—I mean by that one that has stood the
test of experiment,—than that which Fourier extolled ? the participation of the labourers in the profits, this leading them to become
eventually co-proprietors in enterprises and transforming them
from wage-earners into partners ?

Perhaps we shall have the surprise of seeing realised, at least
in part, and before long, that one of all the ideas of Fourier
which seemed the most extravagant—namely, consumption in
common. We see it dawning, this new communism, at the two
extremities of the social ladder, at the top and at the bottom :—
for the wealthy classes it is the life of hotels, boarding-houses,
clubs, which tends to become more general in consequence of
various causes ; it may be, as in the United States, because of the
almost utter impossibility of obtaining domestics, it may be
because of bachelor habits and the progressive dissolution of
family ties :—for the poor classes it is the economic kitchens
which constitute one of the forms of consumption in common ;
they do not necessarily sit at the same table, but they get their food
out of the same pot. There are, too, employees' associations,
which are now being organised, frequently under the patronage
of the administration, in the great postal and telegraph departments for example, and whose object it is to enable the employees

to live at a much smaller cost by being supplied from one common kitchen. I will not say that this aspect of the future is a very joyous one. An odious perspective, on the contrary! the life of the hotel and the *table d'hôte*, if they are to become the general and inevitable rule, will render existence intolerable. The family hearth has, indisputably, already paled ; it no longer blazes as it did in the societies of old where pious hands fed its flame with oil and incense; but it still diffuses a little light and heat, and it would not be without a great loss to humanity that we should see it totally extinguished. But whether this evolution tempt or repel us, it is none the less on its way, and though we may cherish some ill-will towards Fourier for having praised it too highly, old bachelor as he was, we must admire the clear-sightedness with which he predicted it so far in advance.

Finally, if we reduce the system of Fourier to its most general conception; that is to say, if we figure the world to ourselves covered by a net-work of autonomous associations engaged in production for their own use, and exchanging directly with each other the products of their labour, —it cannot be well said that a formula could be found which would better define the social order of the future. Bold indeed would he be who should pretend to determine what the real future will be, but there is ground for the belief that it will present at least certain features of this picture. A considerable number of economists, or moderate socialists, or even philosophers, believe that " free co-operative association is the future." [1] And in fact we already see, in England on a great scale, in other countries in smaller proportions, great co-operative societies being organised, forming a federation with each other and producing for their own use a part at least of the enormous quantity of products which they consume ; they are even beginning to invest the surplus of their capital in agricultural enterprises intended to supply them with the alimentary commodities of which they stand in need. Up to the present, the development of these associations has suffered no break, and if

[1] Secrétan, " Etudes sociales," p. 176.—Hertzka, " Die Gesetze der socialen Entwickelung."—See also our article, " L'avenir de la Co-operation." (*Revue Socialiste*, June, 1888.)

this progression continues, we may look forward to the day when these associations will be the law in the market, and will constitute the new type of economic organisation.

IV

THE school of Fourier has never had the *éclat* of that of Saint-Simon ; but it has perhaps left a more profound trace.   It has counted fewer disciples, but they have remained more faithful.

It was shortly after the publication of the great "Traité de l'Association domestique agricole," about 1825, that the first nucleus of the associative school was formed by Just Muiron, Victor Considérant, Godin, Mme. Clarisse Vigoureux, and some others.   About 1832, this little group was increased by the addition of some deserters from the school of Saint-Simon, the most important being Lechevalier and Abel Transon.   It is at this period that the school began the publication of a weekly paper, *Le Phalanstère:* later on they even organised courses in which lectures were given by MM. Adrien Berbrugger, Considérant, Transon, Philippe Hauger, and sometimes by the master himself.

The death of Fourier, which took place in 1837, gave a new impetus to his doctrines,—a thing of not infrequent occurrence. The school continued to grow in importance up to 1848, at which period it reckoned, it is said, as many as 3700 members, among them the future emperor, Prince Louis Napoleon.   After the revolution of 1848, it was submerged by the great anti-socialist reactionary movement which characterised the second empire. The journal *Le Phalanstère*, which since 1834 had borne the name of *La Phalange*, ceased to appear in 1850.   And it might have been thought that the school would gradually disappear along with the few men who still represented it.   But, by a turn of events quite unexpected, it seems that in these last years the associative school shows a tendency to be restored to a new life. And what is remarkable is that this movement is not due to the initiative of any of the old disciples of Fourier who still survive. The three most noted, Victor Considérant, Brisbane, and De

Pompery no longer carry on a propaganda. It is new men who have raised the flag of the phalanstery. The *Revue du Mouvement social*, edited by M. Limousin, but which is no longer published, the *Devoir*, the organ of the *Familistère* of Guise, these already had kept up the associative tradition. M. Hippolyte Destrem has lately (in 1888) founded a monthly journal entitled *La Rénovation*, an organ of the associative school, and he proposes to inaugurate not exactly the system of harmony, but at least the social order of guaranteeism, which, according to Fourier's theory, ought to serve as a transition. This new school, too, has organised courses, and its members meet at monthly banquets. From time to time, also, newspaper articles appear which bear the visible marks of the Fourierist spirit. This tendency of mind is assuredly due to the remarkable confirmation which certain predictions of Fourier have received from the economic evolution of our time, notably that concerning the multiplication of intermediaries on one hand, and the creation of agricultural syndicates and co-operative associations of consumers on the other.

Fourier's system has been the object of quite a number of experiments in different countries. The first attempt was made while the author was still living, in 1832. One of his disciples, M. Baudet Dulaury, founded a society on shares, and bought about 1200 acres of land near Rambouillet, in Condé-sur-Vesgres, in order to establish a phalanstery, but they did not succeed in raising the necessary capital, and the enterprise was abandoned before they had been able even to begin operations.—For the rest, Fourier repeatedly expressly disowned this attempt, as not fulfilling the conditions circumstantially laid down by him. It is probable that he would likewise have disclaimed all responsibility for the failures which have followed, and it must be admitted that he would in some measure have a right to do so, his system being composed of a series of extremely complicated gearings (he was fond of using this very term), so that if a single wheel is suppressed the entire mechanism is brought to a stand-still.

Some attempts were made in Algeria, but above all in the United States. There, in 1852, thanks to the propaganda of

Albert Brisbane, of Greeley, editor of the New York *Tribune,* of Charles A. Dana, George Ripley and some others, Fourierist ideas had a rapid spread. Three large associations, applying to a greater or lesser extent the principles of Fourierism, sprang into existence almost simultaneously : *The North American Phalanx,* founded by Brisbane in the state of New Jersey, *The Wisconsin Phalanx,* in the state of the same name, and the most famous of all, *Brook Farm* near Boston, which counted very distinguished men among its members, some of whom later took a leading part in the organisation which called itself " Sovereigns of Industry," in the " Knights of Labour," and in the co-operative movement. Even Channing and Hawthorne spent some time there. Thirty of these communities were reckoned in all ; but none of them lasted more than five or six years.[1]

Only a few months ago there was formed, in France, a *" League for Social Progress "* (*Ligue du progrès social*), born of the same impulse for a Fourierist revival of which I have just spoken, its object being to establish an associative colony. We have not heard that it has as yet reached the stage of active operation.

I shall perhaps be reproached with having thus far said nothing of the only experiment which has reflected credit upon the school of Fourier,—the famous familistère of Guise, founded by M. Godin, and which, contrary to pessimist predictions, seems destined to survive its founder. But we have already seen that M. Godin—while applying the system of Fourier in certain details, such as the congregation of the workmen in one " palace," the institution of the nursery (*" poupannat "*), the participation of labour in the profits and by degrees in the ownership itself of the enterprise—has nevertheless diverged from the master upon the essential points. The influence of the doctrines of Fourier upon the establishment at Guise is, however, incontestable, but it is not more direct than that which they have exercised over a great many other co-operative institutions.

It was impossible in the publication of the works of Fourier to

[1] See for most of these details the work of Mr. Richard T. Ely, " The Labour Movement in America."

employ the same method that has been followed for the most part in the volumes already published in this collection, that is, to give his chief work in its entirety, or at least its most important chapters. Fourier's ideas are found thrown pell-mell and without order in all his books. We have therefore found it necessary to ransack the seven or eight voluminous works of his which have been published, to cut out all the passages which have seemed to us to detach themselves from the surrounding mass, either by their superior interest or by giving the most exact expression of the author's idea, and to arrange all these fragments, one after another, classifying them by chapters and by the nature of the subject-matter, so as to give, as far as possible, the impression of a continuous whole. Nevertheless, since we have not permitted ourselves to add connecting remarks, this little book will necessarily have a certain air of disjointedness,—and we could not, for the rest, have deprived it of this character without entirely distorting the work of Fourier, which is distinguished, as we know, by the use of "*l'ordre dispersé.*"—In making a selection of these extracts one might easily have given a caricature of Fourier by reproducing, by preference, as has been done by Louis Reybaud, the most extravagant passages : it would, on the other hand, have been easy to present a highly flattered Fourier by systematically excluding everything of an eccentric character : we have endeavoured to keep equally distant from both of these preconceptions by presenting a realistic Fourier, that is to say, a Fourier fantastic but practical.

We have distributed our chapters, which, we repeat, are composed of bits and fragments, and whose titles are not taken from Fourier, in the following manner :

The first five (Theodicy, Evolution, Rôle of the Passions, Relation of the Sexes, Education) represent what may be termed the philosophical part of Fourier's work.

The four following (Vices of Civilisation, Commerce, Agriculture, Manufactures) represent the critical part : the most interesting for us, because it is that which most closely touches political economy.

The last chapters contain a systematic and practical exposition of the work of Fourier.

At the end of each of these extracts a reference will be found to the work, volume, and page from which it was taken. For these references we have thought it best to direct the reader not to the original editions, bearing the autograph signature of Fourier, and which have now become very rare, but to the later editions which have been published by the school and may be readily obtained in the market. The following is a list of these works.

"Théorie des Quatre Mouvements."—1 vol., 2nd edition, 1841. *Librairie sociétaire.*—(The original edition appeared in 1808 in Lyons, under the false name of Leipsic.)—We refer to it by the abbreviation Q. M.

"Théorie de l'Unité Universelle."—4 vol., 2nd edition. *Librairie sociétaire*, 1838.—(The original edition was published in 1822 in Paris by Bassange, under the title of "L'Association domestique agricole"[1].)—Abbreviation U. U.

"Le Nouveau Monde industriel et Sociétaire."—1 vol., 3rd edition.—*Librairie sociétaire*, 1848.—(The first edition appeared in 1829.)—Abbreviation N. M.

"La Fausse Industrie." 2 vol.—1835-1836.—In the case of this book, from which we have however abstracted but little, we refer, by way of exception, to the original edition.—Abbreviation F. I.

"Manuscrits de Fourier."—*Librairie Phalanstérienne*, 1851.— Abbreviation Man.

There have also appeared in the journal *La Phalange*, from 1845 to 1850, a considerable number of unpublished fragments of Fourier, of which some were off-printed, and a certain number have been collected into a quarto volume, published in 1850, under the title of "*Phalange.*"—But we have made no extracts

---

[1] The school did wrong to change this title which was very happily chosen, while the second is purely oratorical. It may, it is true, justify itself by the authority of Fourier himself, who, in the preface to his book (U. U., i., 4), says : "I have selected the most modest title, but, according to proper procedure, this book should have been entitled 'Théorie de l'unité universelle,' a science touched upon by Newton, who explained one branch of it. . . ."

from these last publications, which are little more than rough drafts which the author used in composing the above-mentioned works.

It goes without saying that, aside from unavoidable suppressions, we have scrupulously reproduced the text, even leaving some errors in orthography, and that the passages in italics, in particular, are so in the original.

Selections from the Works of Fourier

PART FIRST

CHAPTER I

THEODICY

We shall inevitably be led astray unless we adopt as a guide in our researches the five primordial properties of God :

Integral direction of movement.

Economy of means.

Distributive justice.

Universality of providence.

Unity of action.

According to the first, *Integral direction of movement*, the harmonic Groups and Series must draw by attraction the entire body of men to productive labour.

According to the second, *Economy of means*, the Groups must establish in industry and intercourse the greatest combination possible, in opposition to the civilized system which is based upon the smallest possible, the married couple.

According to the third, *Distributive justice*, the régime of the free and harmonic Groups must guarantee a proportional distribution, a graduated minimum, and agreement in distribution.

According to the fourth, *Universality of providence,* this order of things must extend and be applicable to all nations, for the providence of God would be imperfect if he had devised a social system which should not satisfy the needs and secure the happiness of every people, age, and sex.

According to the fifth, *Unity of action,* collective and individual interest must harmonise, so that the individual will be following the right path in yielding blindly to his passions ; otherwise he will be at strife with himself, in accordance with civilised morals. —(Man., 129.)

On beholding this mechanism, or even in making an estimate of its properties, it will be comprehended that *God has done well all that he has done,* and that instead of madly losing thirty centuries in insulting attraction, which is the work of God, the world should have devoted, as I have done, thirty years to its study. —(N. M., 26.)

What could have been God's motives in foregoing to give us a code *supported by attraction?* What motive could he have had in denying it to us? Concerning this hiatus there are six possible opinions.

1° *Either he was unable* to give us a social code of attraction, justice, truth, and unity ; in that case he is unjust in creating this need within us without possessing the means to satisfy us, as he does the animals for whom he institutes social codes which are attractive and regulate the industrial system.

2° *Or he did not wish* to give us this code ; in that case he is premeditatedly a persecutor, creating in us wantonly needs which it is impossible for us to gratify, since none of our codes can extirpate the seven lympic scourges.

3° *Or he was able and did not wish :* in that case he is an emulator of the devil, able to do right and preferring the reign of evil.

4° *Or he did wish and was unable :* in that case he is incapable of governing us, knowing and wishing the right which he is unable to do, and which we are still less able to perform.

5° *Or he neither wished nor was able :* in that case he is inferior to the Devil, who is a scoundrel, but is not stupid.

6° *Or he was able and did wish :* in that case the code exists and he must have revealed it to us ; for of what use would this code be if it were to remain hidden from the people for whom it is designed ?—(U. U., ii., 252.)

CHAPTER II

HUMANITY in its social career has thirty-six periods to pass through; I give below a table of the first, which will suffice for the matter contained in this volume:

LADDER OF THE FIRST AGE OF THE SOCIAL WORLD.

Periods anterior to industry.	K. Bastard, without man. 1. Primitive, termed Eden. 2. Savage state or inertia.
Industry divided up, repulsive.	3. Patriarchism, small industry. 4. Barbarism, medium industry. 5. Civilisation, large industry.
Industry associative, attractive.	6. Guaranteeism, semi-association. 7. Sociantism, simple association. 8. Harmonism, composite association.

I make no mention of the ninth and the following periods because we are not able at present to elevate ourselves beyond the eighth which, itself, is an infinitely happy one when compared with the four existing states of society. It will spread suddenly and spontaneously over the whole of the human race, owing simply to the influence of profit, pleasure, and, above all, industrial attraction,—a mechanism with which our statesmen and moralists are quite unacquainted.—(N. M., 11.)

Each of these periods is subdivided into phases. The following are the phases of civilisation:

INFANCY OR FIRST PHASE.

Ascending Vibration.

Simple   germ,   -   Exclusive marriage or monogamy.
Composite   „   -   Patriarchal or aristocratic feudalism.
         PIVOT,   -   -   *Civil rights of the wife.*
Counterpoise,   -   -   Great federated vassals.
         Tone,   -   -   Chivalric illusions.

ADOLESCENCE OR SECOND PHASE.

Simple   germ,   -   Communal privileges.
Composite   „   -   Cultivation of arts and sciences.
         PIVOT,   -   -   *Enfranchisement of labourers.*
Counterpoise,   -   -   Representative system.
         Tone,   -   -   Illusions of liberty.

APOGEE OR PLENITUDE.

Germs : nautical art, experimental chemistry.
Characteristics : clearing of land, fiscal loans.

VIRILITY OR THIRD PHASE.

Descending Vibration.

Simple   germ,   -   Mercantile and fiscal spirit.
Composite   „   -   Joint-stock companies.
         PIVOT,   -   -   *Maritime monopoly.*
Counterpoise,   -   -   Anarchical commerce.
         Tone,   -   -   Economic illusions.

DECAY OR FOURTH PHASE.

Simple   germ,   -   Municipal pawn-shops.
Composite   „   -   Trade privileges, limited in number.
         PIVOT,   -   -   *Industrial feudalism.*
Counterpoise,   -   -   Farmers of feudal monopolies.
         Tone,   -   -   Illusions of association.

(N. M., 387.)

Our destiny is to advance ; every social period must progress towards the one above it: it is Nature's wish that barbarism should tend towards civilisation and attain to it by degrees; that civilisation should tend to guaranteeism, that guaranteeism should tend to simple association, and so of the other periods. The same is true of phases: the first must tend towards the second, this to the third, this again to the fourth, this to the transition state, and so on in succession. If a society lingers too long in a period or phase, it engenders corruption like stagnant water. (This rule is subject to certain exceptions for the periods inferior to civilisation.)

It is only during the past hundred years that we have been in the third phase of civilisation; but in this short space of time the phase has advanced very rapidly, owing to the colossal progress of industry; so that to-day the third phase exceeds its natural limits. We have too much material for a stage so little advanced; and, this material not finding its natural employment, there is a consequent overloading and discomfort in the social mechanism. This results in a fermentation which taints it; it develops a great number of malevolent characteristics, symptoms of lassitude, effects of the disproportion which exists between our industrial means and the inferior stage to which they are applied. We have too much industry for a civilisation so little advanced, detained in the third phase; it is besieged by the need of raising itself at least to the fourth; thence arise the properties of exuberance and deterioration, of which I shall enumerate the most salient.— (N. M., 418.)

We shall not follow the right path until we establish guaranteeism. It is a stratagem which ought to be employed to oppose liberalism, a stationary spirit which is incapable of advancing, and which is enamoured of a characteristic of the second phase, the *representative system*, a little scheme good in a small republic such as Sparta or Athens, but altogether illusory in a vast and opulent empire like France.—(N. M., 388.)

Every society has a greater or less admixture of characteristics taken from superior or inferior periods; the French, for instance, have lately adopted the *unity of industrial and administrative relations ;* this method, which is one of the characteristics of the sixth period, was introduced by the uniform metric system and the civil code of Napoleon, two institutions opposed to the civilised Order, one of whose characteristics is the *incoherence of industrial and administrative relations.* We have, then, on this point, *deviated from Civilisation and worked into the sixth period.* We have worked into it on other points also, notably by *religious toleration.* The English, who practise a degree of intolerance worthy of the twelfth century, are in this respect more civilised than we. The Germans likewise are more civilised than we as regards the incoherence of laws, customs, and industrial relations ; in Germany one encounters at every turn different measures, sorts of money, laws, and usages, by which means a stranger is robbed and cheated far more easily than if there were but one kind of measure, money, code, etc. This chaos of relations is favourable to the mechanism of civilisation, which seeks, as its aim, to raise knavery to the highest point ; and this would be attained by fully developing the sixteen special characteristics of civilisation.

Nevertheless philosophers maintain " that civilisation has been raised by the adoption of religious toleration, industrial and administrative unity." That is expressing one's self very poorly ; they should have said that *the social Order has been raised and Civilisation lowered ;* in reality, if all the sixteen characteristics of the sixth period were successively adopted it would result in the total annihilation of Civilisation,—it would be destroyed under the belief that it was being perfected. The social Order would be better organised, but the fifth would have been replaced by the sixth period. These distinctions of characteristics lead to an amusing conclusion : it is that *the little good to be found in the Civilised Order is due only to features that are contrary to Civilisation.—*(Q. M., 127.)

The associative [1] Order will fulfil the wish of the nations, by securing to all progressive wealth, the object of everyone's desire: as

---

[1] The word " associative" seems to be better fitted than any other English word to convey the meaning implied by Fourier's term " *sociétaire,*" and has been used as the equivalent of that term in this translation.—Tr.

for Civilisation, from which we are going to emerge, far from its being the industrial destiny of man, it is but a passing scourge with which most of the planets are afflicted during their first ages; it is for the human race a temporary malady, like teething for infants ; it has been prolonged two thousand five hundred years too long througn the inadventence or the pride of the sophists who have disdained all investigation of Association and Attraction ; in fine, the Savage, Patriarchal, Barbarous, and Civilised forms of society are but the thorny paths, the ladders which are to lead us up to the social state which is the destiny of Man, and outside of which all the efforts of the best rulers are unable in any way to remedy the ills of mankind.

It is in vain, then, Philosophers, that you accumulate libraries to search for happiness, while the root of all the social ills has not been eradicated,—*industrial parcelling* or incoherent labour which is the antipodes of God's designs.   You complain that Nature refuses you the knowledge of her laws : well ! if you have, up to the present, been unable to discover them, why do you hesitate to recognise the insufficiency of your methods and to seek new ones ? Either Nature does not desire the happiness of man, or your methods are reproved by her, since they have not been able to wrest from her the secret which you are endeavouring to obtain. Do you see her refractory to the efforts of physicists as she is to yours ?   No, for they study her laws instead of dictating laws to her ; and you only study to stifle the voice of Nature, to stifle the Attraction which is the interpreter of her designs, since it leads on every hand to domestic-agricultural Association.

What a contrast, therefore, between your blunderings and the achievements of the exact sciences ! Each day you add new errors to the old ones, while each day sees the physical sciences advancing upon the road of truth and shedding a lustre upon modern times equal to the opprobrium which has been cast upon them by the visions of regeneration of the sophists.—(U. U., ii., 128, 129.)

CHAPTER III

ALL those philosophical whims called duties have no relation whatever to Nature; duty proceeds from men, Attraction proceeds from God; now, if we desire to know the designs of God, we must study Attraction, Nature only, without any regard to duty, which varies with every age, while the nature of the passions has been and will remain invariable among all nations of men.— (Q. M., 107.)

The learned world is wholly imbued with a doctrine termed MORALITY, which is a mortal enemy of passional attraction.

Morality teaches man to be at war with himself, to resist his passions, to repress them, to believe that God was incapable of organising our souls, our passions wisely; that he needed the teachings of Plato and Seneca in order to know how to distribute characteristics and instincts. Imbued with these prejudices regarding the impotence of God, the learned world was not qualified to estimate the natural impulses or passional attractions, which morality proscribes and relegates to the rank of vices.

It is true that these impulses entice us only to evil, if we yield to them individually; but we must calculate their effect upon a body of about two thousand persons socially combined, and not upon families or isolated individuals: this is what the learned world has not thought of; in studying it, it would have recognised that as soon as the number of associates (*sociétaires*) has reached 1600, the natural impulses, termed attractions, tend to form series of contrasting groups, in which everything incites to industry, become attractive, and to virtue, become lucrative.[1]— (N. M., 125.)

[1] MORALITY looks upon duplicity of action as the necessary state and

The passions, believed to be the enemies of concord, in reality conduce to that unity from which we deem them so far removed. But outside of the mechanism termed "*exalted*," *emulatory, interlocked* (*engrenées*) *Series*, they are but unchained tigers, incomprehensible enigmas. It is this which has caused philosophers to say that we ought to repress them; an opinion doubly absurd inasmuch as we can only repress our passions by *violence* or *absorbing replacement*, which replacement is no repression. On the other hand, should they be efficiently repressed, the civilised order would rapidly decline and relapse into the nomad state, where the passions would still be malevolent as with us. The virtue of shepherds is as doubtful as that of their apologists, and our utopia-makers, by thus attributing virtues to imaginary peoples, only succeed in proving the impossibility of introducing virtue into civilisation.—(U. U., iii., 33.)

We are quite familiar with the five *sensitive* passions tending to Luxury,[1] the four *affective* ones tending to Groups; it only remains for us to learn about the three *distributive* ones whose combined impulse produces *Series*, a social method of which the secret has been lost since the age of primitive mankind, who were unable to maintain the Series more than about 300 years.—(Q. M., 118.)

The four *affective* passions tending to form the four groups of friendship, love, ambition, paternity or consanguinity are familiar enough ; but no analyses, or parallels, or scales have been made of them.

The three others, termed distributive, are totally misunderstood,

immutable destiny of man.   It teaches him to resist his passions, to be at war with them and with himself ; a principle which puts man in a state of war with God, for his passions and instincts come from God, who has given them as a guide to man and to all creatures.—(U. U., i., Avant-propos, 27.)

Its companion, *Metaphysics*, is no less blind and mischievous.   In the study of man it has conceived everything the wrong way ; disregarding the great questions of destiny, the designs of God, and the object of attraction, the interpreter of God, it has engulfed itself in the controversy of the ME, which it has treated only in the *simple* mode.   It should have divided the *me* into simple motive or personal egoism, an *inhuman me*, a germ of discord and vice ; and composite motive or multiple corporative egoism ; this is the *human me*, germ of harmony and virtue, mainspring of balanced distribution in the body of industrial series of a social phalanx.—(F. I., 498.)

[1] Fourier means by this the five senses.—Ch. G.

and bear only the title of VICES, although they are infinitely precious; for these three possess the property of forming and directing the series of groups, the mainspring of social harmony. Since these series are not formed in the civilised order, the three distributive passions cause disorder only. Let us define them.[1]—(U. U., i., 145.)

10th. THE CABALIST is the passion that, like love, has the property of confounding ranks, drawing superiors and inferiors closer to each other. Everyone must recall occasions when he has been strongly drawn into some path followed with complete success.

For instance : electoral cabal to elect a certain candidate ; cabal on 'Change in the stock-jobbing game ; cabal of two pairs of lovers, planning a *partie carrée* without the father's knowledge ; a family cabal to secure a desirable match. If these intrigues are crowned with success, the participants become friends ; in spite of some anxiety, they have passed happy moments together while conducting the intrigue ; the emotions it arouses are necessities of the soul.

Far removed from the insipid calm whose charms are extolled by morality, the cabalistic spirit is the true destination of man. Plotting doubles his resources, enlarges his faculties. Compare the tone of a formal social gathering, its moral, stilted, languishing jargon, with the tone of these same people united in a cabal : they will appear transformed to you ; you will admire their terseness, their animation, the quick play of ideas, the alertness of action, of decision ; in a word, the rapidity of the spiritual or material motion. This fine development of the human faculties is the fruit of the cabalist or tenth passion, which constantly prevails in the labours and the reunions of a passionate series.

[1] Ut.	Friendship.	Violet.	Addition.	Circle.	Iron.
Mi.	Love.	Blue.	Divison.	Ellipse.	Tin.
Sol.	Paternity.	Yellow.	Subtraction.	Parabola.	Lead.
Si.	Ambition.	Red.	Multiplication.	Hyperbola.	Copper.
Re.	*Cabalist.*	Indigo.	Progression.	Spiral.	Silver.
Fa.	*Alternating.*	Green.	Proportion.	Quadratrix.	Platinum.
La.	*Composite.*	Orange.	Logarithms.	Logarithmic.	Gold.
Ut.	UNITYISM.	White.	Powers.	Cycloid.	Mercury.

As it always results in some measure of success, and as its groups are all precious to each other, the attraction of the cabals becomes a potent bond of friendship between all the sectaries (sectaires), even the most unequal.—(U. U., iv., 339.)

The general perfection of industry will spring, then, from the passion which is most condemned by the philosophers ; the cabalist or dissident, which has never been able to obtain among us the rank of a passion, notwithstanding that it is so strongly rooted even in the philosophers themselves, who are the greatest intriguers in the social world.

The cabalist is a favourite passion of women ; they are excessively fond of intrigue, the rivalries and all the greater and lesser flights of a cabal. It is a proof of their eminent fitness for the new social order, where cabals without number will be needed in every series, periodical schisms, in order to maintain a movement of coming and going among the sectaries of the different groups.

But why these innumerable intrigues, some philosopher will ask ; why not make all men brothers, all united in opinion, all enemies of perfidious wealth ?

Why ? It is because man must be provided with springs of action suitable to the social state for which God has destined us. If he had created us for the family and dissociated state, he would have endowed us with soft and apathetic passions, such as philosophy desires. In studying the serial mechanism, it will be seen that the spirit of cabal is its most active principle. God, in order to fit us for the play of the social Series, had to endow us with a strong inclination for cabal.

Accordingly, men, in all deliberative assemblies became pronounced cabalists. The Deity mocks at them when they address a stupid prayer to him to make them all brothers, all united in opinion, according to the wish of Plato and Seneca. God answers them : " Thousands of millions of years ago I created the passions such as the unity of the universe demanded ; I shall not change them to please the philosophers of an imperceptible globule, which must continue, like all the others, subject to the twelve passions, and particularly to the tenth, the cabalist."

12th. THE COMPOSITE.—This passion requires in every action a composite allurement or pleasure of the senses and of the soul, and consequently the blind enthusiasm which is born only of the mingling of the two kinds of pleasure. These conditions are but little compatible with civilised labour, which, far from offering any allurement either to the senses or the soul, is only a double torment even in the most vaunted of work-shops, such as the spinning factories of England where the people, even the children, work fifteen hours a day, under the lash, in premises devoid of air.

The composite is the most beautiful of the twelve passions, the one which enhances the value of all the others. A love is not beautiful unless it is a composite love, combining the charm of the senses and of the soul. It becomes trifling or deception if it limits itself to one of these springs. An ambition is not vehement unless it brings into play the two springs, glory and interest. It is then that it becomes capable of brilliant efforts.

The *composite* commands so great a respect, that all are agreed in despising people inclined to simple pleasure. Let a man provide himself with fine viands, fine wines, with the intention of enjoying them alone, of giving himself up to gormandising by himself, and he exposes himself to well-merited gibes. But if this man gathers a select company in his house, where one may enjoy at the same time the pleasure of the senses by good cheer, and the pleasure of the soul by companionship, he will be lauded, because these banquets will be a composite and not a simple pleasure.

If general opinion despises simple material pleasure, the same is true as well of simple spiritual pleasure, of gatherings where there is neither refreshment, nor dancing, nor love, nor anything for the senses, where one enjoys oneself only in imagination. Such a gathering, devoid of the *composite* or pleasure of the senses and the soul, becomes insipid to its participants, and it is not long before it " grows bored and dissolves."

11th. THE PAPILLONNE [Butterfly] or *Alternating*. Although eleventh according to rank, it should be examined after the twelfth, because it serves as a link between the other two, the tenth and the twelfth. If the sessions of the series were meant to be prolonged twelve or fifteen hours like those of civilised workmen, who, from morning till night, *stupefy themselves* by being engaged in insipid duties without any diversion, God would have given us a taste for monotony, an abhorrence of variety. But as the sessions of the series are to be very short, and the enthusiasm inspired by the composite is incapable of being prolonged beyond an hour and a half, God, in conformity to this industrial order, had to endow us with the passion of *papillonnage*, the craving for periodic variety in the phases of life, and for frequent variety in our occupations. Instead of working twelve hours with a scant intermission for a poor, dull dinner, the associative state will never extend its sessions of labour beyond an hour and a half or at most two ; besides, it will diffuse a host of pleasures, reunions of the two sexes terminating in a repast, from which one will proceed to new diversions, with different company and cabals.

Without this hypothesis of associative labour, arranged in the order I have described, it would be impossible to conceive for what purpose God should have given us three passions so antagonistic to the monotony experienced in civilisation, and so unreasonable that, in the existing state, they have not even been accorded the rank of passions, but are termed only vices.[1]

A series, on the contrary, could not be organised without the permanent co-operation of these three passions. They are bound to intervene constantly and simultaneously in the serial play of intrigue. Hence it comes that these three passions could not be

---

[1] The mania for variety or *papillonnage* may indeed be a vice in the civilised order, which is one incompatible with Nature ; but this passion is none the less an evident necessity in all the kingdoms : breeds need change, alternation, crossing ; in default of which they degenerate. The soil, likewise, demands a change of products and even of seeds ; for a grain will not flourish in the soil that has produced it ; it will succeed better in a neighbouring field. Our stomachs stand in equal need of this *papillonnage ;* a periodic variety of food sharpens the appetite and facilitates digestion.

discerned until the invention of the serial mechanism, and that up to that time they had to be regarded as vices. When the social order for which God has destined us shall be known in detail, it will be seen that these pretended vices, *the Cabalist, the Papillonne, the Composite,* become there three pledges of virtue and riches; that God did indeed know how to create passions such as are demanded by social unity; that He would have been wrong to change them in order to please Seneca and Plato; that on the contrary human reason ought to strive to discover a social condition which shall be in affinity with these passions. No moral theory will ever change them, and, in accordance with the rules of the duality of tendency, they will intervene for ever to lead us TO EVIL in the disjointed state or social limbo, and TO GOOD in the *regime* of association or serial labour.—(U. U., iii., 405-411.)

The seven "affective" and "distributive" passions depend more upon the spirit than upon matter; they rank as PRIMITIVES. Their combined action engenders a collective passion or one formed by the union of the other seven, as white is formed by the union of the seven colours of a ray of light; I shall call this thirteenth passion *Harmonism* or *Unityism;* it is even less known than the tenth, eleventh, and twelfth, of which I have not spoken.

Unityism is the inclination of the individual to reconcile his own happiness with that of all surrounding him, and of all human kind, to-day so odious. It is an unbounded philanthropy, a universal good-will, which can only be developed when the entire human race shall be rich, free, and just.—(Q. M., 121.)

Questions regarding gallantry and the love of eating are treated facetiously by the Civilised, who do not comprehend the importance that God attaches to our pleasures. Voluptuousness is the sole arm which God can employ to master us and lead us to carry out his designs; he rules the universe *by Attraction and not by Force;* therefore the enjoyments of his creatures are the most important object of the calculations of God.—(Q. M., 237.)

I shall, in order to dispose others to share my confidence

explain the object of one of these impulses, accounted as vicious.

I select a propensity which is the most general and the most thwarted by education : it is the gluttony of children, their fondness for dainties, in opposition to the advice of the pedagogues who counsel them to like bread, to eat more bread than their allowance.

Nature, then, is very clumsy to endow children with tastes so opposed to sound doctrines ! every child regards a breakfast of dry bread as a punishment ; he would wish for sugared cream, sweetened milk—food and pastry, marmalades and stewed fruit, raw and preserved fruit, lemonades and orangeades, and mild white wines. Let us observe closely these tastes which prevail among all children ; on this point a great case is to be adjudged : the question to be determined is who is wrong, God or morality ?

God, dispenser of attraction, gives all children a liking for dainties : it was in his power to give them a liking for dry bread and water ; it would have suited the views of morality ; why then does he knowingly militate against sound civilised doctrines ? Let us explain these motives.

God has given children a liking for substances which will be the least costly in the associative state. When the entire globe shall be populated and cultivated, enjoying free-trade, exempt from all duties, the sweet viands mentioned above will be much less expensive than bread ! the abundant edibles will be fruit, milk-foods, and sugar, but not bread, whose price will be greatly raised, because the labour incident to the growing of grain and the daily making of bread is wearisome and little attractive ; these kinds of labour would have to be paid much higher than that in orchards or confectioneries.

And as it is fitting that the food and maintenance of children should involve less expense than those of their parents, God has acted judiciously in attracting them to those sweetmeats and dainties which will be cheaper than bread as soon as we shall have entered upon the associative state. Then the sound moral doctrines will be found to be altogether erroneous concerning the nourishment of children, as well as upon all other points which oppose attraction. It will be recognised *that God did well what he did*, that he was right in attracting children to milk-foods, fruit, and sweet pastries ; and that, instead of foolishly losing three thousand years in declaiming against God's wisest work, against the distribution of tastes and passionate attractions, it would have been better to study its aim, by reckoning with all those impulses combined, which morality insults singly, under the pretext that they are hurtful to the civilised and barbarous orders ; this is true, but God did not create the passions for the civilised and barbarous orders. If he had wished to maintain these two forms of society exclusively, he would have given children a fondness for dry bread, and to the parents a love of poverty, since that is the lot of the immense majority of mankind in civilisation and barbarism. —(N. M., 23.)

In the civilised state, love of eating does not ally itself to industry because the *labouring* producer does not enjoy the commodities which he has cultivated or manufactured. This passion therefore becomes an attribute of the idle ; and through that alone it would be vicious, were it not so already by the outlay and the excesses which it occasions.

In the associative state love of eating plays an entirely opposite *rôle ;* it is no longer a reward of idleness but of industry ; because there the poorest tiller of the soil participates in the consumption of choice commodities. Moreover, its only influence will be to preserve us from excess, by dint of variety, and to stimulate us to work by allying the intrigues of consumption to those of production, preparation, and distribution. Production being the most important of the four, let us first state the principle which must guide it ;. it is the generalisation of epicurism. In point of fact :

If the whole human race could be raised to a high degree of gastronomic refinement, even in regard to the most ordinary kinds of food, such as cabbages and radishes, and everyone be given a competence which would allow him to refuse all edibles which are mediocre in quality or treatment, the result would be that every cultivated country would, after a few years, be covered with delicious productions ; for there would be no sale for mediocre ones, such as bitter melons, bitter peaches, which certain kinds of soil yield, upon which neither melons nor peaches would be cultivated ; every district would confine itself to productions which its soil is capable of raising to perfection ; it would fetch earth for spots where the soil is poor, or perhaps convert them into forests, artificial meadows, or whatever else might yield products of good quality. It is not that the passionate Series do not consume ordinary eatables and stuffs ; but they desire, even in ordinary things such as beans and coarse cloth, the most perfect quality possible, in conformity to the proportions which Nature has established in industrial attraction.

The principle which must be our starting-point is, *that a general perfection in industry will be attained by the universal demands and refinement of the consumers, regarding food and clothing, furniture and amusements.*—(N. M., 253.)

Of what service would the great perfection of culture in every variety of production be to the Harmonians if they had to deal with a public moral and uniform in its tastes, eating only to moderate their passions, and forbidding themselves all sensual refinement, for the benefit of repressive morality. In that case, the general perfection of products would decline from lack of appreciation, the cabalistic spirit would lose its activity among the groups of producers and preparers, agricultural industry would sink back into rudeness, such as we have to-day, when we find scarcely a hundredth part of the civilised capable of judging of the excellence of a commodity ; as a consequence, a vendor who deals in false wares has ninty-nine chances of selling against one of rejection : that is why all provisions are so poor in civilisation.

To obviate this disorder, the associative state will train children to the cabalistic spirit in three directions : in consumption, preparation, and production. It will accustom them from an early age to develop and direct their taste in regard to every dish, every savour, and every form of preparing food ; to exact in the most insignificant viands modes of cooking varied in accordance with the various tastes ; to form, in short, the cabalistic scale in consumption, which will result in its being extended to the work of preparing, preserving, and producing.—(N. M., 71.)

In the civilised order, where labour is repugnant, where the people are too poor to participate in the consumption of choice foods, and where the epicure is not a cultivator, his epicurism lacks a *direct* bond with cultivation ; it is nothing but sensuality, *simple* and ignoble, as is all else which does not attain to *composite* mechanism, or the influence of production and consumption acting upon the same individual.—(U. U., iii., 50.)

The argument would be the same for each of the passions which you term vices. You will recognise by the theory of the combined order that all our characteristics are good and judiciously distributed, that we ought to develop and not correct Nature.[1]

Starting from this principle, we must conclude that the greater the number of pleasures and the more often they are varied, the less shall we be able to abuse them, for pleasures, like labour, become a pledge of health when practised in moderation. A dinner of an hour, diversified by animated conversation which precludes haste and gluttony, will necessarily be moderate, and serve to restore and augment our energies, which would be exhausted by a long repast, liable to be immoderate, such as our great dinners in civilisation.

Harmony, which will offer, particularly to the rich, a choice of pleasures every hour, nay, even every quarter of an hour, will prevent all excesses by the mere fact of the multiplicity of enjoyments ; their frequent succession will be a guarantee of moderation and health. Thenceforth everyone will gain in vigour in proportion to the number of his amusements,—an effect contrary to that produced by them in the civilised mechanism, where the most voluptuous class is everywhere the one soonest deprived of vigour. We must not lay the blame of this upon pleasures but upon the *rarity of pleasures*, which gives rise to excesses which

[1] See the following chapter on *Education.*

seem to justify the moralists in condemning an epicurean mode of life.

Sanitary order, or equilibrium and moderation in the use of our senses, will spring, then, from the very abundance of pleasures which to-day are so pernicious on account of the excesses provoked by their rarity.—(U. U., iii., 155.)

My theory confines itself to *utilising the passions now condemned, just as Nature has given them to us and without in any way changing them.* That is the whole mystery, the whole secret of the calculus of passionate Attraction. There is no arguing there whether God was right or wrong in giving mankind these or those passions; the associative order avails itself of them without changing them, and as God has given them to us.—(U. U., iv., 157.)

Its mechanism produces co-incidence in every respect between individual interest and collective interest, in civilisation always divergent.

It makes use of men as they are, utilising the discords arising from antipathies, and other motives accounted vicious, and vindicating the Creator from the reproach of a lacuna in providence, in the matter of general unity and individual foresight.

Finally, it in nowise disturbs the established order, limiting itself to trial on a small scale, which will incite to imitation by the double allurement of quadruple proceeds and attractive industry.—(F. I., 497.)

CHAPTER IV

OF EDUCATION

THERE is no problem upon which people have gone more astray than upon public instruction and its methods. Nature has, in this branch of social politics, taken a malign pleasure in all ages in confounding our theories and their exponents, from the time of the disgrace incurred by Seneca, the instructor of Nero, to that of the failures of Condillac and Rousseau, of whom the first fashioned only a political idiot and the second did not dare to undertake the education of his own children.—(U. U., iv., 1.)

Man is a being made for Harmony and for all kinds of association : God has furnished him at every period of life with inclinations adapted to the resources and methods offered by the associative state. With us these resources are lacking for the child as well as the grown man ; and as a child deprived of speech is unable to explain itself, it is of all ages the one which suffers most by the absence of the associative *régime*. Infancy, being less provided with reason than the more advanced ages, is so much the more dependent upon the instincts, which, under existing conditions, are allowed no scope. It avenges itself by cries, for its subjection to an education opposed to Nature, cries wearing to the parent and hurtful to the child. Here, then, are two discontented beings instead of two happy ones such as would be produced by associative education. Thus even in the tender age of infancy we meet with this grievous property of civilisation : the engendering of a double evil instead of the double good which was destined for us by Nature.—(U. U., iv., 65.)

Aversion to all useful industry ;
Hatred and derision of superiors ;
Mischievous plotting for destruction ;
Instinct for subjugating and deceiving parents.

This is the civilised child, this the work of philosophy. Were it not *à propos* here to say with Beaumarchais, "how stupid brilliant people are"? (*"que les gens d'esprit sout bêtes."*)—(U. U., iv., 35.)

Civilisation is obliged constantly to employ one of the two minor groups, that of the family, to criticise the child and try to set it right. The result of this is a double cross-purpose in the domestic bond ; on one side, irritation and secret rebellion of the child, which follows a law of Nature in disdaining the criticism of the parent and preceptor; on the other, annoyance and frustration of the parent, who, reluctantly fulfilling a painful duty, obtains as his reward only the indifference of the child. These disagreeable features disappear completely in Harmony, where the child, frequenting thirty groups and series, meets a throng of friends and sectaries, rigid censors of his incompetence : their frankness quite absolves the parent from remonstrance.—(U. U., iii., 347.)

Thereupon great uprising of parents and philosophers.

"You wish, then," they will exclaim, "to take the child away from its natural teacher, who is the father?" I do not wish anything. I do not follow the practice of the sophists who promulgate their silly whims in education as laws, such as the mania of plunging a child in winter into cold water, in order to imitate some republicans of antiquity. I confine myself to analysing the designs of Attraction.—(U. U., iv., 31.)

It will be observed that in Harmony the only paternal function of the father is to yield to his natural impulse, to spoil the child, to humour all his whims.

The child will be sufficiently reproved and rallied by his peers. When an infant or little child has in the course of the day passed through half a dozen such groups and undergone their jokes, he is thoroughly imbued with a sense of his insufficiency, and quite disposed to listen to the advice of the patriarchs and venerables who are good enough to offer him instruction.

It will, after that, be of little consequence that the parents at the child's bed-time indulge themselves in spoiling him, telling him that he has been treated too severely, that he is really very charming, very clever ; these effusions will only skim the surface, they will not convince. The impression has been made. He is humbled by the railleries of seven or eight groups of little ones which he has visited during the day. In vain will it be for the father and mother to tell him that the children who have repulsed him are barbarians, enemies of social intercourse, of gentleness and kindliness ; all these parental platitudes will have no effect, and the child on returning to the infantile seristeries the following day will remember only the affronts of the day before ; it is he who in reality will cure the father of the habit of SPOILING, by redoubling his efforts and proving that he is conscious of his inferiority.—(U. U., iv., 33.)

Harmonic education tends by its methods first of all to develop instinctive vocations from the very earliest age, to fit every individual for the different functions for which Nature has destined him, and from which he is diverted by the methods of civilisation, which, save in rare exceptions, employ everyone in a capacity contrary to his vocation.

"If at birth your star has made you a poet," the teachings of morality and filial duty will tend to make you, as was the case with Metastasio, a porter instead of a poet, and all the apparatus of philosophic wisdom will be set in motion to draw you into occupations from which Nature wished to keep you aloof. Nine-tenths of the civilised could give vent to this complaint.

There is no question, therefore, more obscure among us than that of vocation or the instinct of social functions. This problem will be fully cleared up by the mechanism of harmonic education. It never develops a single vocation in the child, but thirty graduated vocations, with varying degrees of dominance.—(U. U., iv., 3.)

Nature endows every child with a great number of instincts in industry, about thirty, of which some are primary or guiding and lead to those that are secondary.

The point is to discover first of all the primary instincts : the child will seize this bait as soon as it is presented to him ; accordingly, as soon as he is able to walk, to leave the infant seristery, the male and female nurses in whose charge he is placed hasten to conduct him to all the workshops and all the industrial reunions which are close by ; and as he finds everywhere diminutive tools, an industry in miniature, in which little tots of from two and a half to three years already engage, with whom he is anxious to associate, to rummage about, to handle things, at the end of a fortnight one may discern what are the workshops that attract him, what his industrial instincts.

The phalanx containing an exceedingly great variety of occupations, it is impossible that the child in passing from one to the other should not find opportunities of satisfying several of his dominant instincts ; these will exhibit themselves at the sight of the little tools manipulated by other children a few months older than himself.

According to civilised parents and teachers, *children are little idlers;* nothing is more erroneous ; children are already at two and three years of age very industrious, but we must know the springs which Nature wishes to put in action to attract them to industry *in the passionate series and not in civilisation.*

The dominant tastes in all children are :

1. *Rummaging* or inclination to handle everything, examine everything, look through everything, to constantly change occupations ;

2. Industrial *commotion*, taste for noisy occupations ;

3. *Aping* or imitative mania.

4. Industrial *miniature*, a taste for miniature workshops.

5. *Progressive attraction* of the weak toward the strong.

There are many others ; I limit myself to naming these five first, which are very familiar to the civilised.   Let us examine the method to be followed in order to apply them to industry at an early age.

The male and female nurses will first exploit the mania for rummaging so dominant in a child of two. He wants to peer into every place, to handle and examine everything he sees. He is consequently obliged to be kept apart, in a bare room, otherwise he would destroy everything.

This propensity to handle everything is a bait to industry; to draw him to it, he will be conducted to the little workshops; there he will see children only two and a half and three years old using little tools, little hammers. He will wish to exercise his imitative mania, termed APING; he will be given some tools, but he will want to be admitted among the children of twenty-six and twenty-seven months who know how to work, and who will repel him.[1]

He will persist if the work coincides with any of his instincts : the nurse or the patriarch will teach him some portion of the work, and he will very soon succeed in making himself useful in

[1] A property general among children is *aping* or the *imitative mania*. They wish to try what they see others doing who are more advanced in years. It is upon this fancy, termed *ascending tone*, that almost the entire system of attractive education of little children and infants will be grounded.

The mania referred to is powerfully developed by permitting them to behold the manœuvres in Harmony, such as these evolutions :

Soldiers at drill ;
Censer-bearers in procession ;
Dancers at the Opera.

Let twenty little children or "tots" be gathered together at random. If they are given a chance to see these various manœuvres, they will all be eager to imitate them. In default of a gun, they will each of them take a stick ; in default of a censer, a stone suspended from a string ; in default of a crook, the branch of a willow.

If they should be given little guns, little censers, little crooks, you will see them transported with joy, listening with respectful docility to the instructions in evolution which a little cherub of six will be good enough to impart to them. Their enthusiasm will be still more heightened if they should be furnished in addition with costumes and paraphernalia, if they should be given little grenadier caps, little surplices for the procession, little reeds for the choregraphic figures.—(U. U., iv., 28.)

some trifling things which will serve him as an introduction ; let us examine this effect in regard to an inconsiderable kind of labour, within the reach of the smallest children,—the shelling and sorting of green peas. This work which with us would occupy the hands of people of thirty, will be consigned to children of two, three, four years of age : the hall is provided with inclined tables containing a number of hollows ; two little ones are seated at the raised side ; they take the peas out of the shell, the inclination of the table causes the grains to roll towards the lower side where three tots are placed of twenty-five, thirty, thirty-five months, charged with the task of sorting, and furnished with special implements.

The thing to be done is to separate the smallest peas for the sweetened ragout, the medium ones for the bacon ragout, and the largest for the soup. The child of thirty-five months first selects the little ones which are the most difficult to pick out ; she sends all the large and medium ones to the next hollow, where the child of thirty months shoves those that seem large to the third hollow, returns the little ones to the first, and drops the medium grains into the basket. The infant of twenty-five months, placed at the third hollow, has an easy task ; he returns some medium grains to the second, and gathers the large ones into his basket.

It is in this third rank that the infant *débutant* will be placed ; he will mingle proudly with the others in throwing the large grains into the basket ; it is very trifling work, but he will feel as if he had accomplished as much as his companions ; he will grow enthusiastic and be seized by a spirit of emulation, and at the third *séance* he will be able to replace the infant of twenty-five months, to send back the grains of the second size into the second compartment, and to gather up only the largest ones, which are easily distinguished.—(N. M., 181.)

If civilised education developed in every child its natural inclinations, we should see nearly all rich children enamoured of various very plebeian occupations, such as that of the mason, the carpenter, the smith, the saddler. I have instanced Louis the XVI. who loved the trade of locksmith ; an Infanta of Spain preferred that of shoemaker; a certain king of Denmark gratified himself by manufacturing syringes; the former king of Naples loved to sell the fish he had caught in the market-place himself; the prince of Parma, whom Condillac had trained in metaphysical subtilties, in the understanding of intuition, of cognition, had no taste but for the occupation of church-warden and lay-brother.

The great majority of wealthy children would follow these plebeian tastes, if civilised education did not oppose the development of them; and if the filthiness of the workshops and the coarseness of the workmen did not arouse a repugnance stronger than the attraction. What child of a prince is there who has no taste for one of the four occupations I have just mentioned, that of mason, carpenter, smith, saddler, and who would not advance in them if he beheld from an early age the work carried on in bright workshops, by refined people, who would always arrange a miniature workshop for children, with little implements and light labour?—(U. U., iii., 543.)

No attempt will be made, as is the case in existing educational methods, to create precocious little *savants*, intellectual primary school beginners, initiated from their sixth year in scientific subtilties; the endeavour will by preference be to secure mechanical precocity; capability in bodily industry, which, far from retarding the growth of the mind, accelerates it.

If one wishes to observe the general inclination of children of from four and a half to nine years of age, he will see that they are strongly drawn to all material exercises, and very little to studies; it is right then, that, in accordance with the desire of nature or attraction, the cultivation of the material should predominate at that age.

Why this impulse of childhood toward material exercises? Because Nature wishes, above all, to make man husbandman and manufacturer, to lead him to wealth before leading him to science.—(U. U., iv., 73, 74.)

The point is to determine what influence may be exerted over the physical constitution of children and the developments of the human body by *an integral play of the faculties and attractions of the soul, combined with the integral exercise of the faculties of the body by means of proportional gymnastics.*—(U. U., iv., 188.)

Associative education regards the body of the child as an accessory and coadjutor of the soul. It looks upon the soul as upon a great lord who will not enter his castle until the intendant has put all the roads in proper order. It begins by moulding the body at an early age to all the uses which will be conformable to the harmonic soul, that is to say, to *justice*, to *truth*, to *combinations*, and to UNITY.

And in order to accustom the body to all these "perfections" before moulding the mind, two resources quite foreign to our present methods are brought into play ; they are, among others, the OPERA and COOKERY. Let us demonstrate that there is nothing arbitrary in this selection, that it is methodically obligatory.

Of the five senses there is one, that of *touch*, whose influence is almost null before the age of puberty. A child does not know love, the chief branch of the sense of touch ; for the rest, he is quite indifferent regarding the other pleasures pertaining to touch, being satisfied with a wooden seat, a bed of rushes, coarse cloth ; he disdains a stuffed arm-chair, a soft bed, costly furs. The niceties of touch have no value whatever in his eyes, but he is strongly inclined to the enjoyments of the other four senses which he should exercise.

the two active ones *taste and smell*, by COOKERY :
the two passive ones *sight and hearing*, by the OPERA.

These are the two points to which attraction guides him ; children and cats would forever be haunting the kitchen, if they were not chased away. As for the magic of the opera, and visible fairy-land, there is nothing more enticing for a child.—(U. U., iv., 76.)

Now, when seven-eighths of the children are devoted to playing in opera and to busying themselves with cooking, will they be worth less on that account ? That is what we are going to investigate.

Let us observe, first, that in order to make a perfect agriculturist of the child, as regards the management of animal and vegetable products, he must be initiated very early in the refinements of that cooking, that gastronomy, proscribed by the fierce lovers of radishes and " black broth."—(U. U., iv., 104.)

We remark everywhere that the class which is the most temperate at table is that of cooks ; they are generally epicures, severe judges, partaking indeed of all the dishes, but without going to any excess. They are proportionally the most sober of the classes that have access to good cheer without limit.

The best preservative against gluttony, then, for children as well as parents, would be an order of things where they would all become *cooks* and *refined gourmands*, otherwise called *gastronomes*. As regards the opera, being with us nothing but an arena of gallantry and an allurement to expenditure, it is not to be wondered at that it is reprobated by the moral and religious class ; but in harmony it is an amicable reunion, free of charge ; it cannot be the occasion of any vicious intrigues between people who meet each other every moment in the various occupations of the industrial series.—(U. U., iv., 79.)

CHAPTER V

OF THE CONDITION OF WOMEN [1]

EVERY period has a certain characteristic which forms the *pivot of mechanism*, and the absence or presence of which determines the change of periods. This characteristic is always derived from love. In the fourth period it is the *absolute servitude of woman ;* in the fifth period it is *exclusive marriage and civil liberties of the wife;* in the sixth period it is the *amorous corporation* which ensures women the privilege of which I have spoken above. If a barbarous people adopted *exclusive marriage,* they would in a short time become civilised through this innovation alone ; if we adopted the *seclusion and sale of women,* we should in a short time become barbarous through this single innovation ; and if we adopted the *amorous guarantees,* we should find in this single measure an exit from civilisation and an entrance into the sixth period.

If God has endowed amorous customs with such great influence upon the social mechanism and upon the metamorphoses which it is capable of undergoing, this must be a consequence of his horror of oppression and violence ; he desired the well-being or the misery of human societies to be proportional to the constraint or freedom which they would allow. Now God recognises as freedom only that which is extended to both sexes and not to one alone ; he desired, likewise, that all the seeds of social abominations such as savagery, barbarism, civilisation, should have as their sole pivot the subjection of women, and that all the seeds of social well-being such as the sixth, seventh, eighth

1 See chap. ii. on *Evolution.*

periods should have no pivot but the progressive enfranchisement of the weak sex.—(Q. M., 131.)

As a general proposition : *Social advances and changes of periods are brought about by virtue of the progress of women towards liberty, and the decadences of the social order are brought about by virtue of the decrease of liberty of women.*

Other events influence these political vicissitudes ; but there is no cause which so rapidly produces social progress or decline as a change in the condition of women. I have already said that the adoption of closed harems would of itself soon transform us into barbarians, and the opening of the harems would of itself cause a people to pass from barbarism to civilisation. To sum up, *the extension of privileges to women is the general principle of all social progress.*—(Q. M., 195.)

It is not always an advantage to introduce a characteristic of a higher period ; it may in certain cases become perverted by this political transplanting, and produce evil consequences ; witness *free divorce,* which is a characteristic of the sixth period, and which has produced so much disorder in civilisation that it has been necessary to assign to it the narrowest limits. Nevertheless, free divorce is a very salutary custom in the sixth period, and there contributes eminently to domestic harmony ; for it is there combined with other characteristics which do not exist in civilisation. We may see by this, that discretion must be employed in introducing a characteristic of one period into another, just as in transporting a plant into a climate not its own.[1] It was a

---

[1] "All these new regenerators, Owen, Saint-Simon, and others, are strongly inclined to speculate upon the emancipation of women ; they do not understand that before making any changes in the established order regarding the relations of love, many years are needed to create guarantees which do not now exist. . . . On the other hand, modifications in the regulation of love will only be applicable to a polished generation, educated entirely in the New Order, and faithful to certain laws of honour and delicacy which the Civilised make a sport of violating. A man is applauded in France if he succeeds in deceiving women and husbands ; the morals of the Civilised are a sink of vice and duplicity. A generation trained to such usages could not but abuse an extension of liberty in love. . . ."

"And when the admission of these liberties would be suitable as far as fortune and manners are concerned, they will be introduced only *by degrees* and not suddenly. . . . Each liberty will be admitted only after it shall have been

mistake to suppose that unlimited religious toleration could be fitted for the civilised ; in the long run, it would produce in agricultural states more evil than good if it did not accept religions which are characterised by the morals of the fourth, third, and second periods, such as Mohammedanism, Judaism, and idolatry.   As for the present, their admission is a matter of indifference, since civilisation is drawing to its close.—(Q. M., 129.)

I do not mean to criticise civilised education here, or to insinuate that we ought to inspire women with a spirit of liberty. Assuredly, it is necessary that each social period should fashion its youth to reverence the dominant absurdities ; and if in the barbarous order it is necessary to brutalise women, to persuade them that they have no souls, so as to dispose them to allow themselves to be sold in the market or shut up in a harem, it is likewise necessary in the civilised order to stupefy women from their infancy, so as to make them fit the philosophic dogmas, the servitude of marriage, and the debasement of falling into the power of a husband whose character will perhaps be the opposite of theirs.   Now, since I should blame a barbarian who trained his daughters for the usages of the civilised state in which they will never live, I should likewise blame a civilised man who trained his daughters in a spirit of liberty and right peculiar to the sixth and seventh periods, which we have not attained.[1]

If I accuse the prevailing education and the servile spirit with

voted for throughout the entire globe, by the fathers and husbands ; then it may be believed to be useful.   The effect of these liberties will be a powerful contribution to the charm of labour, the increase of production, and the reign of loyal morals ; but in civilisation we should witness only the production of the three opposite effects."   (1831, *Pièg et Charl. des deux sect S.-Sim. et Ow.*, p. 53).—(Q. M., 155.)

[1] To speak plainly, the fathers play a vile *rôle* in civilisation when they have any daughters to marry off.   I can conceive how paternal affection may blind them to the infamy of the manœuvres and cajoleries to which they resort in order to entice marriageable men ; but they can at least not blind themselves as to the anxieties and contemptibleness of such a *rôle*.   How ardently ought those who are overburdened with daughters to desire the invention of a new domestic Order, where marriage no longer exists, and where one is relieved of the care of providing girls with husbands, and what fervent thanks do they owe him who brings them this invention !—(Q. M., 168.)

which it inspires women, I speak in relation to other societies where it will be unnecessary to pervert their character by force of prejudices. I indicate to them the distinguished position they might attain, following the example of those who have overcome the influences of education and resisted the oppressive system which the conjugal tie necessitates. In pointing to those women who have succeeded in spreading their wings, from viragos like Maria Theresa to those of a milder shade, like the Ninons and the Sévignés, I am justified in saying that woman in a state of liberty will excel man in all functions of the mind or the body which are not the attributes of physical force.

Already does man seem to have a premonition of this; he becomes indignant and alarmed when women belie the prejudice which accuses them of inferiority. Masculine jealousy has burst forth above all against women writers; philosophy has eliminated them from academic honours and thrust them ignominiously back to household concerns.

Was not this affront the proper due of learned women? The slave who wishes to ape his master merits from him only a glance of contempt. What concern had they with the vulgar glory of composing a book, of adding a few volumes to the millions of useless ones already in existence? What women were called to produce was not writers but liberators, a political Spartacus, geniuses who would devise means for raising their sex from degradation.

It is upon women that civilisation weighs; it was for women to attack it. What is their existence to-day? They live only by privation, even in industry, where man has invaded everything down to the petty occupations of sewing and the pen, while women are to be seen drudging at the painful labours of the field. Is it not scandalous to see athletes of thirty stooping over a desk, or transporting a cup of coffee with their shaggy arms, as if women and children were lacking to attend to these trifling duties of the desk and the household?

What, then, are the means of subsistence for women without a fortune? The distaff or it may be their charms, if they possess any. Yes, prostitution more or less veiled is their sole resource, and philosophy denies them even that ; this is the abject fate to which they are reduced by that civilisation, that conjugal slavery, which they have not even thought of attacking. That was the only problem worthy of engaging women writers ; their indolence in regard to it is one of the causes which have increased man's contempt. Slavery is never more contemptible than when by a blind submission it convinces the oppressor that his victim is born for slavery.—(Q. M., 220, 221.)

Civilised love, in marriage, is, at the end of a few months, or perhaps the second day, often nothing but pure brutality, chance coupling, induced by the domestic tie, devoid of any illusion of the mind or of the heart : a result very common among the masses where husband and wife, surfeited, morose, quarrelling with each other during the day, become necessarily reconciled upon retiring, because they have not the means to purchase two beds, and contact, the brute spur of the senses, triumphs a moment over conjugal satiety. If this be love, it is a love most material and trivial.

And yet this is the snare upon which philosophy reckons to transform the most gracious of the passions into a source of political dupery, to excite the rapid growth of population, and stimulate the poor by the sight of their progeny in rags. What a noble *rôle* assigned to love, in exchange for the freedom ravished from her ! She is made among the civilised a provider of food for cannon ; and among barbarians, a persecutor of the weaker half of humanity : these are, under the names of harem and marriage, the honourable functions which are assigned to love by our pretended lovers of liberty !

Confounded by the vices of their love-polity, they repel every suggestion of estimating the properties of free love. Ignorant and deceitful as to the proper uses of liberty, they desire it to be unlimited in commerce, where crime and roguery everywhere require the curb of the law ; and they deprive love of all liberty— love, whose vast scope in the passionate series would lead to all virtues, to all wonders in social politics. What an unlucky science they make, these civilised theories ; what an instinct of opposition to all the desires of nature and of truth !— (U. U., iv., 462.)

PART SECOND

CHAPTER VI

OF THE VICES OF CIVILISATION

AUTHORS of the uncertain sciences, who pretend to labour for the good of the human race, do you believe that six hundred million barbarians and savages form ¬o part of the human race? Yet they suffer; well, what have you done for them? Nothing. Your systems are only applicable to civilisation.

Far from succeeding in civilising and uniting the human race, your theories gain only the profound contempt of the barbarians, and your customs excite only the irony of the savage; his strongest imprecation against an enemy is to wish him our fate, and to say to him : " May you be reduced to working a field!" Words which may be regarded as a malediction uttered by Nature itself. Yes, civilised industry is reproved by Nature, since it is abhorred by free peoples who would embrace it at once if it accorded with the passions of man.—(Q. M., 408.)

If industry has made some progress in Europe, has it not lost immense regions in Asia ? If Civilisation has founded in America feeble colonies, already threatened with decadence by the revolt of the negroes, has it not lost at the gateway of Europe the vastest empires—Egypt, Greece, Asia Minor, Carthage, Chaldea, and a part of Western Asia? Industry has been stifled in extensive and beautiful countries like Bactriana, where it was beginning to be introduced ;

the empire of Samarkand, famous of old in the Orient, and all the regions stretching from the Oxus to the mouths of the Indus, have retrograded politically and reorganised the Horde.— (Q. M., 411.)

However, social order, in spite of the impotence of such guides, yet makes some progress, such as the suppression of slavery ; but what slowness in conceiving and executing the right ! Twenty centuries of science elapsed before the least alleviation of the lot of the slave was proposed ; thousands of years, then, are needed to open our eyes to a truth, to suggest an act of justice ! Our sciences, which boast their love of the people, are totally ignorant of the means of protecting them.

It is to chance, therefore, and not to the political and moral sciences that we owe our feeble advances in the spirit of society ; but chance makes us purchase each discovery with centuries of stormy trials. The movement of our societies may be compared to that of the sloth, whose every step is counted by a groan ; like it, civilisation advances with an inconceivable slowness through political torments ; with each generation it tries new systems which only serve, like briers, to stain with blood those who take hold of them.—(Q. M., 148, 149.)

It is, above all, in industrial policy that our century displays its pride ; proud of some material strides, it does not perceive that it is retrograding politically, and that its rapid advance is that of the crab, which moves, but moves backward.

Industrialism is the latest of our scientific chimeras ; it is the mania of producing in confusion, without any system of proportional compensation, without any guarantee to the producer or wage-earner that he will participate in the increase of wealth ; accordingly, we find the industrial regions sprinkled with beggars to as great, or, perhaps, a greater extent than those countries which are indifferent to this sort of progress.

Let us judge systems here by their results ; it is England that is the point aimed at, the model offered to the nations, the object of their jealousy ; in order to estimate the happiness of its people, I shall fortify myself by unexceptionable testimony.

Assembly of master-workmen of Birmingham, March 21, 1827. It declares "that the industry and frugality of the working man are unable to shield him from want, that the mass of wage-earners employed in agriculture are destitute ; that they actually die of hunger in a country where there is a superabundance of food." Testimony all the less open to suspicion in that it proceeds from the class of foremen who are interested in justifying the wages of the working-men and disguising their wretchedness.

Here is a second witness, equally interested in concealing the weak side of his nation ; it is an economist, an industrialist, who is going to denounce his own science.

London, House of Commons, February 28, 1826.

Mr. Huskisson, Minister of Commerce, says : "Our silk factories employ thousands of children who are held in leash from three o'clock in the morning until ten o'clock at night : how much do they get a week ? a shilling and a half, thirty-seven French sous, about *five and a half sous per day,* for being tied down to their work nineteen hours, superintended by foremen provided with whips with which they strike every child that stops for a moment."

This is slavery actually restored : it is evident that the excess of industrial competition leads civilised nations to the same degree of poverty and servitude as the populace of China and Hindustan, most anciently famous by their prodigies in agriculture and manufactures.

Alongside of England let us place Ireland, which, by double excess in extreme cultivation and in sub-division of properties, has arrived at the same condition of destitution which England attains by double excess in manufactures and great estates. This contrast in one and the same empire well demonstrates the vicious circle of civilised industry.

The newspapers of Dublin (1826) say : "There is an epidemic prevailing here among the people : the sick that are taken to the hospital recover as soon as they have been given food." Their sickness, then, is HUNGER : one need not be a sorcerer to divine that, since they are cured as soon as they have something to eat. Have no fear that this epidemic will attack the great : you will

not see either the Lord-Lieutenant or the Archbishop of Dublin
fall ill from hunger, but rather from indigestion.

And in places where the civilised masses do not die of *pressing*
hunger, they die of *slow* hunger through privations, of *speculative*
hunger which constrains them to nourish themselves with unwholesome food, of *imminent* hunger through overwork, through
engaging in pernicious pursuits, enduring excessive fatigue, which
gives birth to fevers, to infirmities.

Our economists, confounded at beholding the tenacity and
even progress of indigence, begin to suspect that their science is
on the wrong track ; a discussion on this subject took place
recently between MM. Say and Sismondi ; the latter, returned
from an inspection of the prodigies beyond the Channel, declared that England and Ireland, with their colossal industry, are
nothing but vast conglomerations of the poor ; that industrialism
up to the present is only a region of chimeras. M. J. B. Say
made a reply defending the honour of the science ; but, to speak
plainly, political economy lost its bearings in the plethoric crisis
of 1826 ; it is trying to justify itself. Already we hear the heads
of the school, as for example the late Dugald Stewart, say that the
science is restricted to a passive *rôle*, that its task is limited to
the analysis of existing evil.

That is to act like a physician who should say to his patient :
" My ministry consists in making an analysis of your fever, and
not in pointing out to you the means of curing it." Such a physician would appear ridiculous to us ; nevertheless that is the *rôle*
that some economists wish to assume to-day ; perceiving that
their science has only succeeded in aggravating the evil, and at a
loss to find an antidote, they say to us, like the fox to the goat :
" Try to get out of it, and use all your efforts."

If we grant this passive *rôle*, this egoism, by which they believe
they excuse the impotence of the science, they will still find great
trouble in keeping their word, in giving the analysis of the evil ;
for they do not wish to acknowledge its extent, to admit that
everything is vicious in the industrial system, that it is every way
a world turned inside out. Let us judge of it by a half-confession

which recently escaped M. Sismondi : he has recognised that consumption operates in an *inverted manner*, that it is based upon the whims of the idle, and not upon the well-being of the producer ; this is at any rate a first step towards analytical sincerity. But this inverted mechanism, is it limited to consumption ? is it not evident :

That *exchange is inverted*, carried on by intermediaries called *merchants, traders*, who, becoming owners of the product, levy tribute upon the producer and the consumer, and sow disorder in the industrial system by their underhand dealings in monopolies, stock-jobbing, cheating, extortion, bankruptcy, etc.

That competition is inverted, tending to the reduction of wages, and leading the people to indigence through the progress in industry ; the more it increases, the more is the labourer obliged to accept very low remuneration for labour too much contended for ; and on the other hand, the more the number of merchants increases, the more are they drawn to cheating, through the difficulty of realising any profit.

Here are already three forces directed in an inverted manner, in the industrial mechanism ; I could readily name thirty of them ; why admit only one, that of inverted consumption ?

Industry offers a subversion far more striking ; this is the *opposition of the two kinds of interest, collective and individual.* Every person engaged in an industry is at war with the mass, and malevolent toward it from personal interest. A physician wishes his fellow-citizens good, genuine cases of fevers, and an attorney good lawsuits in every family. An architect has need of a good conflagration which should reduce a quarter of the city to ashes, and a glazier desires a good hail-storm which should break all the panes of glass. A tailor, a shoemaker, wishes the public to use only poorly-dyed stuffs and shoes made of bad leather, so that a triple amount may be consumed,—for the benefit of trade ; that is their refrain. A court of justice regards it opportune that France continues to commit a hundred and twenty thousand crimes and actionable offences, that number being necessary to maintain the criminal courts. It is thus that in civilised industry every individual is in intentional war against the mass ; necessary result of anti-associative industry or an inverted world. We shall see this absurdity disappear in the associative *régime*, where each individual will find his advantage only in that of the mass.

Of all the indications that ought to make us suspect the industry of to-day, there is none more striking than that of the simple scale of distribution. I mean by *simple*, a scale which increases only on one side and not on the other ; here is an example adapted to the five classes :

	Poor.	Straitened.	Medium.	Easy.	Rich.
A	0	1	2	4	8
B	1	2	4	8	16
C	2	4	8	16	32
D	4	8	16	32	64
E	8	16	32	64	128

Line A represents the beginnings of society, where the difference of fortunes was but little noticeable, where the poor class, denoted by o, did not exist.

According as the public wealth increases, as we see in lines B, C, D, E, the poor class ought to participate in it in the proportion indicated in each of those lines, that is to say that in the degree of wealth marked E, the rich, having 128 francs a day to spend, the poor would have at least 8 francs ; in that case the scale would be composite, increasing in proportion for the five classes, and without equality.

But in civilisation, the scale, increasing only on one side, the poor class always remains at zero, so that when wealth has reached the fifth degree, E, the rich class, receives indeed its share of 128 francs, and the poor only zero ; for it has always less than the necessaries of life ; so that the civilised class follows the transverse line o, 2, 8, 32, 128, and the multitude, or poor class, far from sharing in the increase of wealth, gathers from it only added privations ; for it sees a greater variety of commodities which it cannot enjoy ; it is not even sure of obtaining repugnant labour which is its torment, and which offers no advantage but that of saving it from starvation.

In this respect, indolent nations like the Spanish are more fortunate than industrious ones, for the Spaniard is sure of finding work when it shall please him to accept it. The French, the English, the Chinese, do not enjoy this advantage.

I do not conclude from this that the social *régime* of Spain is laudable, far from it ; I merely wish to reach the point indicated by the heading of this article, to demonstrate that everything is a vicious circle in fragmentary (*morcelé*) or civilised industry ; it creates, by its progress, the elements of happiness, but not happiness itself; that can only be created by the *régime* of industrial attraction and proportional distribution in conformity with line E. This distribution is impossible so long as industry is repugnant ; the masses must continue in extreme destitution in order that they should contrive to carry it on. Besides, civilisation producing hardly a quarter of what would be produced by association, and multiplying in population beyond measure, it would be impossible to secure to these swarms a minimum share, or the real necessities of life.

This vicious circle of industry has been so clearly recognised, that people on all sides are beginning to suspect it, and feel astonished *that, in civilisation, poverty should be the offspring of abundance.*

After having proved that the lot of the civilised masses must of necessity be unfortunate, let us remark that the progress of industry adds little or nothing to the happiness of the rich. The *bourgeoisie* of Paris, to-day, has more beautiful furniture, prettier gew-gaws, than the great of the seventeenth century ; what does that add to happiness ? Our ladies with their Cashmere shawls, are they happier than the Sévignés, the Ninons ? We see at present the petty *bourgeois* of Paris served in vessels of gilded porcelain ; are they happier than the ministers of Louis XIV., the Colberts, the Louvois, who had dishes of earthenware ?

There is beyond doubt real enjoyment in improvements affecting comfort and health such, for example, as the springs of carriages ; but one grows *blasé* after a week regarding the refinements of visual luxury, such as porcelain ; they only serve to excite the cupidity of the poor, who imagine that the wealthy classes find great happiness in the possession of these baubles. They will only be useful in the associative order, where they will have the double property of stimulating industrial attraction and of multiplying the harmonies of the passions, which are indeed a real enjoyment, and which will be shared by the poor, as well as the rich, in spite of the extreme inequality of fortunes. Then the poorest of men will have many more pleasures than the most opulent monarch of to-day, because the order termed passionate Series creates social harmonies or pleasures of the soul, which at present are well-nigh unknown to the great, and it raises sensual refinements to a perfection of which the civilised world is incapable of forming any conception.

Civilised industry, therefore, I repeat, can only create the elements of happiness, but not happiness itself. It will, on the contrary, be demonstrated that excess of industry leads civilisation to very great misfortunes, if the methods of real progress in the social scale are left undiscovered.—(Q. M., 28, 29, 33, 35.)

What is to-day the number of active and positive labourers ? It does not amount to more than a third of the population. I have proved that a labourer, apparently useful, often performs only a *negative* labour, such as a wall of enclosure, which is not a real and positive production.

In the parallel between the labours of civilisation and of Harmony, it will be seen that *null or negative* functionaries constitute TWO-THIRDS of the population ; namely :

TABLE OF NON-PRODUCTIVES IN CIVILISATION.

Domestic parasites.	Social parasites.	Accessory parasites.
	4. Armies.	
1. Women.	5. Fiscal Officials.	9. Stoppage.
2. Children.	6. Manufactures.	10. Sophists.
3. Servants.	7. Commerce.	11. Idlers.
	8. Transportation.	12. Seceders.

Agents of positive destruction.
Agents of negative creation.

DOMESTIC PARASITES.

1° Three-fourths of the WOMEN of cities and half of those of the country, through absorption in the labours of the household and in domestic complications. Accordingly their day is estimated, in economics, at only one-fifth of that of a man.

2° Three-fourths of the CHILDREN, entirely useless in cities and of little use in the country, considering their unskilfulness and their mischievousness.

3° Three-fourths of household DOMESTICS not cultivators, whose labour is only the consequence of complication, particularly in cooking, and half of the servants of the stable, servants of luxury and of the products of luxury, who, being necessary only by reason of industrial division, become superfluous in Association.

These three classes composing the household form a class apart in the series of parasites. They will cease to figure there in the associative order, where judicious distribution, the proper employment of the sexes and of services, will reduce to one-fourth or one-fifth the number of hands brought into requisition to-day by the immense complication of separated households or incoherent families.

SOCIAL PARASITES.

4° The ARMIES of the land and sea, which divert from industry the sturdiest youth and the largest amount of taxes, dispose that youth to depravity, by constraining it to sacrifice to a parasitic function the years which it ought to employ in disposing itself to labour, for which it loses the taste in the military state.

The apparatus of men and machines which is termed an army is employed in producing nothing, waiting to be employed in destruction. This second function will be spoken of later. Here we are considering the army only in its aspect of stagnation.

5° The legions of ADMINISTRATION. We see that in France

the customs alone absorb 24,000 men : add to this the tax-gatherers and other armies of clerks, fieldkeepers, gamekeepers, spies, etc., in fine, all complicated administration, such as that of the finances and others which will be needless in an order where each Phalanx will pay its taxes at a stated time and upon a simple notice from the minister.

6° A full half of the MANUFACTURES reckoned useful, but which are *relatively* unproductive through the poor quality of the things manufactured ; things which upon the hypothesis of general excellence would reduce the present waste and manufacture one-half, and in many instances three-fourths in works undertaken for the Government, which all are agreed to cheat.

7° Nine-tenths of the MERCHANTS and commercial agents, since true commerce, or the associative method, accomplishes this class of service with a tenth of the agents employed in it by the existing complicated order.

8° Two-thirds of the agents of *transportation* by land and sea, who are improperly included in the commercial class, and who, to the vice of complicated transportation, add that of adventurous transportation, notably upon the sea, where their ignorance and improvidence increase the number of shipwrecks tenfold.

Let us place in this category *smuggling*, which often results in making the sum of the movements and agents ten times as great as would be employed in direct transportation. Goods being carried from Dover to Calais have been known to pass through Hamburg, Frankfort, Basle, and Paris; to travel 500 leagues instead of 7, all for the equilibrium of commerce and of perfectibility.

ACCESSORY PARASITES.

STOPPAGES, legal, accidental and secret ; people inactive, be it through lack of work or for the sake of recreation. They would refuse this inaction under the *régime* of attractive labour ; they stretch it on the contrary to double of the legal concessions, desisting from labour on *Saint-Monday*, the most ruinous of all the saints, for he is fêted 52 days a year in manufacturing towns.

Let us add the various *fêtes*—corporation, revolution, carnival, patronage, marriage, and so many others upon which people would not desire to leave off work in an order in which the industrial gatherings will be more agreeable than the feasts and balls of the civilised.

Under abstention from labour we must reckon accidental stoppage. If the master is out of sight, the labourers stop ; if they see a man or a cat pass all are in a stir, masters and servants, leaning upon their spades and gazing in order to divert themselves : forty, fifty times a day do they lose five minutes in that way. Their week hardly amounts to four full days. What an amount of stoppage in the absence of industrial attraction !

10° The SOPHISTS, and, first of all, the controversialists [legists] ; those who read them and mingle at their instigation in party affairs, in unproductive cabals. To controversial labour, which confuses every subject, must be added the political commotions and industrial distractions of which it is the cause.

The list of controversialists and sophists would be far more extensive than one might think, if we spoke of jurisprudence alone, which seems a pardonable sophism ; let us suppose that the associative order does not engender a twentieth part of the present litigations, and that, to settle these few differences, it possesses means as expeditious as ours are complicated ; the conclusion is that nineteen-twentieths of the bar are parasites, as well as the litigants, the witnesses, the journeys, etc., etc. How many other parasites in sophism, beginning with the economists, who inveigh against the body of parasites whose standard-bearers they are.

11° The IDLE, people said to be *comme il faut*, who pass their lives in doing nothing. Let us add to them their valets and the entire class that serves them. One is unproductive if he serves unproductive people, as is the case with the *solliciteurs*, whose number has been reckoned at 60,000 in the city of Paris alone. Let us put into this category the whole *personnel* of elections.

Prisoners form a class in enforced idleness ; the sick still more so.   We shall not see among native harmonians one-tenth of the sick that we see in civilisation.   For, although sickness is an inevitable vice, it is susceptible of correction and of enormous reduction.   Out of ten sick people nine are unseasonably withdrawn from labour, as a consequence of the civilised *régime ;* nine who in the associative state would be in good health,—no offence meant to the physicians.

12° The SECEDERS, people in open rebellion against industry, the laws, morals, and usages.   Such are lotteries, gambling-houses, veritable social poisons, sharpers, prostitutes, vagrants, beggars, pickpockets, brigands, and other seceders, whose number tends less than ever to decrease, and whose suppression obliges the maintenance of a gendarmery and of functionaries equally unproductive.

PIVOTAL CLASSES.

The agents of POSITIVE DESTRUCTION ; those that organise famine and the plague, or contribute to war.   The civilised order accords its high protection to the agents of famine and pestilence ; it cherishes stock-jobbers and Turks ; it encourages every species of invention which may extend the ravages of war, Congreve fusees, Lamberti cannon, etc.[1]

Agents of NEGATIVE CREATION.   I have already proved that they are exceedingly numerous ; that the greater part of work done, such as walls of enclosure, are relatively unproductive ; others are illusory, through misconception or lack of skill ; such as edifices which fall to pieces, bridges and roads which have to be displaced or rebuilt.   Others are an indirect injury : a hundred labourers appear to be accomplishing a useful work by clearing a forest ; they are preparing the ruin of the country, and are more

---

[1] *Note.*—The military figures in this table in two lines ; here, as carrying on war, effecting destruction, and in No. 4, as limited to stagnation, to an unproductive *rôle.*   It is not a double enumeration, but a difference of *rôle,* a double character, which requires two distinct notices.

fatal to it than the ravages of war, which may be repaired. Others are scourges by counter-stroke, lauded by economism, such as the invention of a method which will reduce to beggary a thousand labourers, whose inaction will be a source of disorders.—(U. U., iii., 173-179.)

A good reply to the boastings of civilised perfectibility is a picture of the miseries which philosophy has actually created in the course of a single generation. All those of which you are about to read a long list date back less than forty years : [1]

1° *Progress of financiering,* systems of extortion, indirect bankruptcy, anticipations of revenue, art of devouring the future. Necker did not know in 1788 where to raise 50 millions to cover the annual deficit, but since THE SCIENCE WHICH DID NOT EXIST UNDER NECKER HAS BEEN CREATED, a way has been found to increase not by 50 but by 500 million the annual taxes, which in 1788 did not amount to half a milliard ;

2° *Progress of the mercantile spirit :* consideration accorded to commercial plundering and knavery. Stock-jobbing raised to a power which scoffs at law, encroaches upon all the fruits of industry, shares in the authority of governments, and propagates everywhere the frenzy of gambling in the public funds ;

3° *Concentration.* Capital, transformed into vortexes which absorb all resources, attract all the people of wealth, and cause agriculture to be more and more disdained ;

4° *Maritime Monopoly.* It was contested and restrained in 1788 ; now it is exclusive master, with no chance for the Europeans to re-establish rival navies ;

5° *Heredity of evil,* or custom of adopting vices which have been introduced. Let the Directory establish a scandalous usage, the farming out of public gambling ; its successors will declaim against it, and will maintain the vice. The same is the case in small things and great, from the monopoly of gambling to conscription. The civilised state does indeed make progress, but it is in the art of legalising and accumulating all sorts of disorder ;

[1] Written in 1823.—Ch. G.

6° *Attacks upon property*, degenerating into a habit under pretexts of revolution, pretexts which become rules for succeeding parties ;

7° *Overthrow of intermediary bodies*, provincial Estates, parliaments and corporations, which imposed limits upon the central power. It is thanks to their overthrow that means have been found for an annual supply of five hundred millions, where Necker was unable to draw fifty ;

8° *Spoliation of communes :* among other political evils, it has produced that of *octrois*, a true means of alienating the people of cities and rendering them docile followers of agitators ;

9° *Instability of institutions*, smitten by reason of this with impotence, even where they are wise, thwarted by revolutionary habits which are secretly kept up among people worn out by the excess of taxation ;

10° *Deep-rooted discords ;* local hatred and leavens of dissension, improperly stifled by systems of simple action which suppress the evil instead of absorbing it ;

11° *Destructive or accelerating tactics* which quadruple the ravages of war, cause the revival of barbarous usages, vendettas, guerillas, levies *en masse ;* drag everybody, down to women and children, into war.

12° *Immorality of politics*, the union of Christianity with the Ottomans against a Christian nation which wishes to escape massacre ; a PASSIVE concert for the maintenance of pirates and for traffic in negroes, which could be stopped at once by vigorously punishing the well-known guilty parties ; the shamelessness of commerce, constructing vessels for the Algerians, which will serve to stock their bagnios with Christian slaves.

—DIRECT DEPRAVITY OF THE SCIENCES : obstinate refusal to explore neglected fields of research ; contempt of experience, which shows the sophists the nine scourges as the abiding fruit of their systems ; jugglery of making believe that everything has been discovered, that those who offer inventions should be scoffed at ; mercantile spirit of the learned world, reducing the arts and sciences to a commercial and intriguing gaming-house, crushing everybody who does not enjoy the favour of the philosophical *coteries.*

—INDIRECT DEPRAVITY OF THE SCIENCES; among other things, through progress in chemistry, the achievements of which only serve to plague the poor by furnishing commerce with the means of debasing all commodities: potato bread, wine of Indian wood, sham vinegar, sham oil, sham coffees, sham sugar, sham indigo; everything in provisions and manufactures is but a travesty, and it is the poor man who suffers by this chemical cheapening: he alone is the victim of all these mercantile inventions, which could be made to serve useful ends in a *régime* of genuine relations, but which will grow more and more harmful until the close of civilisation.

CHAPTER VII

OF COMMERCE

COMMERCE at its origin was despised and ignored by the philosophers, who even to-day comprehend it so little that they confound it with the useful class of manufacturers. Commerce did not win the homage of the learned until it was in full triumph, just like the farmers of revenue, whom no one thinks of making much of until they appear in their coach-and-six ; then the orators extol their virtues and devour their fine meals. It is thus that philosophy has behaved in regard to the commercial spirit ; it did not cajole it until it had reached the pinnacle ; before that it did not deem it even worthy of attention. Spain, Portugal, Holland, and England exercised a commercial monopoly for a long time, and philosophy thought neither of praising nor blaming it. Holland succeeded in amassing its immense fortune without seeking any enlightenment from the economists ; their sect was not yet born when the Dutch were already accumulating tons of gold. The philosophers of that time were wholly occupied in diving into beautiful Antiquity, or in " meddling " in religious quarrels.

Finally they perceived that this new policy of commerce and monopoly might furnish matter to fill large volumes and bring a new *coterie* into repute ; it was then that philosophy was seen to give birth to sects of economists, who, notwithstanding their recent origin, have already duly piled up volumes upon volumes, and promise to equal the tomes of their predecessors.—(Q. M., 337.)

Nature is never deceptive in the general impulses which it bestows upon mankind. If the great majority of nations disdain a calling such as commerce, if this disdain is dictated to them by natural instinct, be sure that the object of their contempt contains some odious and hidden property.

Which of the two are the most sensible, the moderns who honour commerce or the ancients who consigned merchants to contempt ? *Vendentes et latrones*, says the Scripture, which puts these two classes together. Thus thought Jesus Christ, who armed himself with scourges to drive out the merchants, and said to them with evangelical frankness : *You have made my house a den of thieves.*

" Fecistis eam speluncam latronum."

In accord with Jesus Christ, beautiful Antiquity confounded merchants and thieves, whom she placed pell-mell under the patronage of Mercury. It seems that at that period the mercantile calling bordered close upon infamy, for Saint-Chrysostom declares that *a merchant cannot be agreeable to God ;* accordingly, merchants are excluded from the Kingdom of Heaven, although the elect of all other vocations are admitted, even an attorney, in the instance of Saint-Ives.

I cite these particulars in order to establish the opinion of the Ancients, which I wish to place in comparison with that of the moderns. I am far from approving this exaggeration of the Ancients ; it was as ridiculous to proscribe and scoff at merchants as it is ridiculous to exalt them to the skies. But which of the two excesses is the less absurd ? I declare in favour of the Ancients.[1]—(Q. M., 337-392.)

The mechanism of commerce is organised in opposition to common sense. It subordinates the social body to a class of parasitic and unproductive agents, the merchants. All the essential classes, the proprietor, the cultivator, the manufacturer,

---

[1] There have been cited as exceptions some small nations of antiquity that devoted themselves to commerce, such as Tyre and Athens. But these nations had no territory: the famous republic of Athens was smaller than the smallest of the eighty-seven provinces of France. Nations without territory like Athens, or restricted to an ungrateful soil like Holland, constitute an exception to the general rule : they engage zealously in parasite industry ; they become corsairs, manufacturers, monopolists, traders. They can readily excuse the mercantile calling which is their sole resource, and to aid which they drained the countries of the producers.—(U. U., ii., 201.)

and even the government, find themselves dominated by an accessory class, that of the merchant, which ought to be their inferior, their commissioned agent, removable and responsible, and which nevertheless directs and obstructs at its pleasure all the forces of circulation.—(Q. M., 332.)

Commerce is the natural enemy of factories; while feigning a solicitude to support them, it really labours only to levy contributions upon them. In the majority of manufacturing cities, accordingly, it is recognised that the small, not very prosperous, manufacturer works only for the dealer in materials; just as it often happens that the small cultivator works only for the usurer, and the little *savant* of the attic for the great *savant* of the Academy, who condescends to publish under his own name the fruit of the vigils of a literary wage-worker.

In brief, the trader is an industrial corsair, living at the expense of the manufacturer or producer. To confound these two functions is to be ignorant of the alphabet of the science.[1]— (U. U., ii., 217.)

Commerce has a goal which has not been caught sight of by the economists; it tends to metamorphose civilisation into industrial feudalism; it tends to establish federative companies, like that of the English Indies, which reduced to bondage the masses and the small proprietors.

Free competition, then, has as its ulterior result *mercantile feudalism.* This order is established by companies enjoying special privileges, which, once organised, govern jointly with the sovereign, share with him the profits of the monopoly, and reduce to industrial slavery all outside of their body. They lay down the law unobstructed, in the general market, by their vast capital. Thenceforth every mediocre proprietor finds himself compelled to submit to the rate of prices prescribed by them. . . . Such is the outcome towards which the mercantile spirit of the noble science

[1] Manufactures being, after agriculture, the principal source of wealth, merchants and bankers being merely accessory agents, servants whose existence depends upon an industry which they do not create, servants who can never be lacking to the factories; policy should favour the manufacturers and not the traders.—(Manuscrits, p. 254.)

of political economy tends. This established order is the last phase of civilisation, which, in accordance with the law of the meeting of extremes, must end as it began, by a feudalism reproduced in the direction opposite to the first.

Without waiting for oppression to reach this point, experience demonstrated to us that free competition has as its end, its visible result, the encroachment upon mediocre fortunes by civilised matadores. To-day, when competition carried to the highest point prevails in France ; to-day, when the streets are lined with merchants and bankers . . . we see them hatching plots every day, to cause a rise in some sort of commodity, and gorging themselves with gold, at the expense of general industry, whose various branches they convulse by turns,—all, the effect of free competition.

The servitude of governments goes on increasing, and the ascendancy of stock-jobbers has reached such a point that the gambling of the Exchange has become the guide of opinion. Do the public funds fall, the common people look upon it as an irrefutable thermometer, and every pigmy draws the conclusion that the ministry is acting amiss. This decline is frequently a result of the intrigues of jobbers more powerful than the minister. What ministry can wrestle with coalitions of stock-jobbers, among whom we see a single individual making 80 millions in one year for himself?

As soon as a cabal can set this spring of political disturbance in motion, this factitious fall of the public funds, opinion in concert throws discredit upon the doings of the cabinet. No more is required to lead to the unseasonable downfall of a ministry, and often the fate of an empire is compromised by the intrigues of the jobbers of the Exchange. Has servitude been ever better demonstrated?

This state of things ought to fasten the attention of science : it is clear that civilisation has assumed a new aspect, that monopoly and stock-jobbing, which are two commercial characteristics, have overthrown the old order. Is this a cause for triumph or for alarm ? *What issue does this monstrous irruption of the mercantile power, whose encroachments go on increasing, presage ?*—(U. U., ii., 205.)

The first thing that men should have noted who seek for truth is that it is banished from commerce.

Another important observation that the aspect of commerce should suggest is that it offers germs of association of various sorts.

Political thought should have based two kinds of speculation upon the commercial mechanism : the one, positive, which should have consisted in developing in it the germs of Association, source of all economy, and in striving subsequently to introduce this into agriculture : the other, negative, which should have tended to banish from the mechanism of commerce that deception which we find there generally prevalent, and which is the strongest bar to activity of intercourse.

The two problems were allied and were soluble by each other's aid ; for guarantees of truth cannot be introduced into commerce without the help of Association, and the social bond cannot be widened without discovering the guarantees of truth.—(U. U., ii., 199.)

One would have augured a reform of this sink of corruption, of this inept mechanism, which, by the concurrence of sixty malevolent characteristics, makes industry a trap for the nations, and aggravates at once their wretchedness and their depravity.   It is maintained that people are not more deceitful than they were formerly ; nevertheless one could, half a century ago, obtain at a reasonable rate goods of a durable colour, and natural foods ; to-day, adulteration, knavery prevail everywhere.   The cultivator has become as great a defrauder as the merchant used to be. Dairy products, oils, wines, brandy, sugar, coffee, flour, everything is shamelessly debased.   The masses can no longer procure natural foods ; only slow poisons are sold them, such progress has the spirit of commerce made even in the smallest villages.— (N. M., 43.)

Forestalling is the most odious of commercial crimes, in that it always attacks the suffering part of industry.   If there is a scarcity of provisions or any other commodities, the monopolists are on the watch to aggravate the evil, to seize upon the existing supplies, to give earnest-money to secure those that are expected, to divert them from circulation, to double, treble the price by under-hand dealings which exaggerate the scarcity and diffuse a fea-which is recognised too late as illusory. They produce the effect in the industrial world of a body of butchers who should go upon the field of battle to aggravate and tear open the wounds of the suffering.

One circumstance that has contributed to the favour which monopolists enjoy to-day, is that they were persecuted by the Jacobins; they emerged from that conflict more triumphant than ever, and he who should raise his voice against them would at first seem an echo of Jacobinism. But do we not know that the Jacobins slaughtered indiscriminately all sorts of classes, whether they were honest men or robbers? did they not send to the same scaffold Hébert and Malesherbes, Chaumette and Lavoisier? And because these four men were sacrificed by the same faction, does it follow that we must assimilate them, and will it be said that Hébert and Chaumette were good men because they were, like Malesherbes and Lavoisier, immolated by the Jacobins? The same reasoning applies to monopolists and stock-jobbers, who, though they were persecuted by the enemies of order, are none the less disorganisers and vultures unchained against honest industry.

They have, nevertheless, found extollers among that class of scholars who are called *economists*, and nothing is, to-day, more respected than monopolism and stock-jobbing, which, in the style of the day, are termed *speculation and banking*, because it is not proper to call things by their names.

One very curious consequence of the civilised order is the fact that if classes evidently mischievous, such as that of the monopolists, *are repressed* directly, the evil becomes still greater, *commodities become scarcer*, and this was convincingly shown under the reign of terror. It is this that has caused philosophers to conclude that *merchants must be left alone—"Laisser faire les marchands.*" Comical remedy for an evil, to maintain it because no antidote is known ! It should have been sought for, and, until it was discovered, their underhand dealings condemned instead of lauded : encouragement should have been held out for the quest of a method capable of repressing them (associative competition).—(Q. M., 354.)

The fault of which I am about to speak is not scandalous like the preceding one, but it is not less injurious.

In an age in which economy has been carried into the most minute details, such as replacing coffee by chicory juice, sugar by the juice of the beet-root, and other means of saving which serve only to promote the trickery of merchants, to provoke travellers, who are unable to procure good things at any price—in an age so parsimonious, I say, how is it that it has not been perceived that the chief economy ought to consist in the *economy of hands* of superfluous agents that could be spared, and that we waste upon unproductive functions, such as those of commerce ?

I have observed that in our practice a hundred men are frequently employed in a piece of work which would require barely two or three if association prevailed ; twenty men would suffice to supply *the market* of a city where, to-day, we find a thousand peasants repairing. We are, as far as regards the industrial mechanism, as raw as a people who should ignore the use of mills, and employ fifty labourers to grind grain which is to-day crushed by a single millstone. The superfluity of agents is frightful everywhere, and generally amounts to four times what is necessary in all commercial employments.

Since philosophy inculcates the love of traffic, merchants are found swarming even in the villages. The heads of families renounce the cultivation of the soil, to devote themselves to itinerant brokerage ; if they have but a calf to sell, they will lose days in loitering about in the market-places and taverns. It is particularly in wine-growing countries that this abuse is seen to prevail ; everywhere, *free competition* raises the number of merchants and commercial agents to infinitude. In large cities like Paris it is reckoned that there are as many as a thousand grocers, while scarcely three hundred would be required to serve adequately the usual needs. The profusion of agents is the same in the small market-towns ; a little town, which to-day receives a hundred commercial travellers and a hundred pedlars in the course of a year, saw, perhaps, less than ten in 1788, and yet there was no lack of either provisions or clothing, at very moderate prices, although the merchants amounted to less than a third of the present number.

This multiplicity of rivals causes them to engage, in emulation of each other, in the maddest enterprises, and such as are most ruinous to the social body ; for every superfluous agent, such as the monks were, for instance, is a despoiler of society, wherein he consumes without producing anything. Is it not recognised that the monks of Spain, whose number is reckoned as high as 500,000, would produce the sustenance of two million persons, if they returned to agriculture ? The same is the case with superfluous traders, whose number is incalculable ; and when you shall understand the commercial method of the sixth period, *associative competition*, you will be convinced that commerce could be carried on with one quarter of the agents it employs to-day, and that there are in France alone *a million* inhabitants abstracted from agriculture by the abundance of agents created by free competition. There is, then, for France alone, an annual loss of the sustenance of four millions of inhabitants, consequent upon an error of the economists.

Besides the waste of hands, the present order causes furthermore a waste of capital and commodities. I cite as an example one of the commonest abuses of to-day, the crushing out of competitors (*l'Écrasement*).

Grown too numerous, the merchants contend desperately for sales which become more difficult every day on account of the abundance of competitors. A city which consumed a thousand tons of sugar when it had ten merchants will continue to consume only a thousand tons when the number of merchants shall have increased to forty instead of ten ; that is what has taken place in all the cities of France. Now we hear this swarm of merchants complain of the dulness of trade, when they should be complaining of the superabundance of merchants ; they ruin themselves by outlays incurred to entice custom, and to overpass rivals ; they venture upon the maddest sorts of expenditure for the pleasure of crushing out their rivals.   It is a mistake to believe that the merchant is dominated by his interest alone : he is in great part a slave of his jealousy and his pride ; some ruin themselves for the barren honour of devising great enterprises, others, for the mania of annihilating a neighbour whose success exasperates them. Mercantile ambition, obscure though it be, is none the less intense, and if the trophies of Miltiades disturbed the slumbers of Themistocles, one may also say that the sales of a shopkeeper disturb the slumbers of his shopkeeping neighbour.   That is the origin of that frenzy of competition which drives so many merchants to their ruin, and causes them to waste their substance in expenditures which ultimately fall back upon the consumer ; for the social body is in the last instance the sufferer by any form of waste.   We had a striking proof of this in the war waged by the stage-coach companies, which, in order to injure each other, would willingly have carried their passengers gratis.   Seeing them lower their rates so as to crush each other, people would remark : *They will soon pay us a premium to carry us post.*   It is important to emphasise these details in order to prove that the economists are grossly mistaken in supposing that interest is the sole motive of the trader.   What sensible man could in cold blood have conceived the idea of carrying passengers post from Paris to Rennes for tenpence ?   Such are the follies produced by the mania of annihilation.   The result of these onsets, amusing to the travellers, was the bankruptcy of the various champions, who were annihilated by each other in the space of a few months.   Their bankruptcy was borne by the public, which is always interested in the wildest enterprises ; and, despite the failure of such undertakings, the bankrupt is the gainer by despoiling those associated with him, whom he does not reimburse for their investments.   That is why merchants, confident of saving themselves by bankruptcy in case of reverses, risk everything to ruin a rival and enjoy a neighbour's misfortune ; they resemble those Japanese who put out one of their own eyes in front of an enemy's door in order to have the law put out both of his.—(Q. M., 373-377.)

Commerce, notwithstanding all these evils, is regarded as a perfect method of exchange, because the contracting parties are free to come to terms or to decline to do so.

This freedom is only a negative bond. It is of no value except by comparison with the methods of barbarians, with requisitions, maximums, tariffs, etc. ; the freedom enjoyed in commerce is far from sufficient in itself to secure in exchanges equity, fidelity, confidence, economy, and other desirable bonds which are incompatible with the commercial order. This order secures all the opposite vices ; it causes the triumph of plunder and roguery ; it disseminates a general mistrust which diminishes intercourse and necessitates expensive precautions ; finally, it causes the whole course of exchange to be slow and complicated.—(Man., 248.)

The merchants are free to-day, but the social body is not so in its relations with them ; for we are compelled to make purchases ; we cannot do without food and raiment, which can only be obtained by purchase ; we are therefore in reality subjected to the vendors, whose knavery we are enforced to endure.

Such a mechanism is only *simple and not reciprocal liberty ;* the liberty is entirely on the side of the vendors, of whom the consumer is the dupe, and against whom he has no guarantee. Such a guarantee ought to be discovered and introduced, in order to raise the commercial *régime* to *composite or reciprocal* liberty.— (U. U., ii., 195.)

The fundamental principle of the systems of commerce, the principle : *Allow perfect liberty to the merchants,* concedes to them absolute ownership of the commodities in which they deal ; they have a right to withdraw them from circulation, to hide, and even to burn them, as has more than once been done by the Oriental Company of Amsterdam, which publicly burned stores of cinnamon in order to raise the price of that article. What it did in the case of cinnamon, it would have done in the case of wheat, had it not been afraid of being stoned by the people ; it would have burned a part of the wheat or allowed it to rot, so as to sell the remainder at quadruple its value. What! Do we not see every day at the docks stores of grain, which have become rotten because the merchant waited too long for a rise, thrown into the sea? I myself have superintended, in the capacity of clerk, such infamous operations, and one day I ordered twenty thousand quintals of rice to be thrown into the sea, which could have been sold at an honest profit before they were spoiled, had the holder been less eager for gain. It is the social body that suffers the loss of such waste, which we find occurring anew every day, under the shelter of the principle: *Let the merchants alone.* ("*Laissez faire les marchands.*")

And if you consider that the company, according to the rules of commercial freedom, has the right of refusing to sell at any price, of allowing the wheat to rot in its granaries, while the people are perishing, can you believe that the starving nation is in conscience bound to die of hunger for the honour of the fine philosophic principle, *Let the merchants alone?* No, surely not; admit, then, that the right of commercial freedom ought to be subject to restrictions corresponding to the needs of the social body; that a person provided with a superabundance of a commodity of which he is neither the producer nor the consumer, ought to be regarded as a CONDITIONAL TRUSTEE, and not as an absolute owner. Admit that merchants or intermediaries of exchange ought to be subordinated in their dealings to the good of the masses, and not be at liberty to clog general intercourse by all those most disastrous manœuvres which are admired by your economists.—(Q. M., 357-359.)

CHAPTER VIII

OF AGRICULTURAL PRODUCTION

WE boast of our advances in agriculture ; they are held up to admiration, being compared with the incapacity of the barbarians : are we, then, on the road to perfection because we are a little less stupid than an ignorant neighbour? If we could behold the productions of the Harmonians at the end of half a century—the length of time necessary to restore the forests, which cannot, like cabbage, be raised in a season—we should be greatly astonished to discover that civilisation, with its jargon of perfectibility, is wholly savage, in various branches of industry, for instance grazing; and that in other branches of great importance, notably water and forests, we fall far below the savages. For we do not, like them, confine ourselves to leaving them uncultivated and in their primitive state; we bring the axe and destruction, and the result is landslides, the denuding of mountain-sides, and the deterioration of the climate.

This evil, by destroying the springs and multiplying storms, is in two ways the cause of disorder in the water system. Our rivers, constantly alternating from one extreme to the other, from sudden swellings to protracted droughts, are able to support only a very small quantity of fish, which people take care to destroy at their birth, reducing their number to a tenth of that which they ought to produce. Thus, we are complete savages in the management of water and forests.

How our descendants will curse civilisation, on seeing so many mountains despoiled and laid bare, like those in the South of France ! [1]—(U. U., iii., 478.)

[1] This society, so vaunted, does not raise its atmosphere to half its possible

We are carried away by the poet's pictures of rural pleasures, and are blind to the miseries of civilised agriculture ; Delille, purity. Italy is full of moors and swamps ; its ridges of the Apennines are exhausted, laid waste, from Genoa to Calabria. France is in a still more disordered state ; the destruction of its forests causes a visible deterioration of climatic condition ; it banishes the orange from Provence ; it is rapidly driving out the olive, and will soon drive out the vine.

It is not thus that the associative order carries on cultivation ; it distributes a universality of cultivation as if the entire globe belonged to one company of shareholders ; it raises every canton, every province, every region to a state of combined perfection ; it undertakes all the general operations of re-planting forests, irrigation, and drainage ; all kinds of works which tend to render the atmosphere, whether local or general, wholesome, milder, and purer.

In this condition of things, the various regions, instead of communicating to each other the germs of storms, exchange only the germs of gentle breezes, waters and forests wisely distributed prevent the excesses at once of heat and of cold ; and the general mildening of the temperature is the outcome of this universal perfection of cultivation. The atmosphere becomes, in that case, refined to the *integral composite* degree, termed *supercomposite*, which requires two springs of perfection : that of *general cultivation* and *judicious distribution* of cultivations.

The triple harvest can result only from this *composite integral* refinement or spreading over all parts of the earth ; and in that case, the advantage of thirty degrees will be general throughout all the continents ; twenty at the two Arctic poles, the frozen region at the north being reduced to one-fourth, that at the south diminished only by half.

Then, a vessel leaving Europe will make a tour of the two passes in eighteen months ; it will skirt the coast of Siberia during the first summer ; it will winter in Behring Strait, taking on the commodities deposited by the fleets of Mexico and of China. The following spring it will pass through Parry Strait and Baffin's Bay, and will return to London at the end of eighteen months employed in the great coasting-trade of Siberia and Arctic America.

Will this perspective be accused of exaggeration? It ceases to arouse suspicion if we start out from a veritable fact, the influence of human cultivation upon atmosphere and climatic conditions. We cannot too often repeat, and we should, like Harpagon, have it graved in letters of gold, *that the air is a field subject, as well as the earth, to industrial exploitation.*

This amelioration is not one of those that may be promised to take place all of a sudden, since it presupposes the complete cultivation of the globe and a full supply of population. But if not suddenly, it will be enjoyed gradually and rapidly ; a hundred and twenty to a hundred and thirty years will suffice to consummate this precious metamorphosis. Each generation will see a very sensible bettering of its climatic conditions, thanks to the power which Association possesses of again covering the mountains with trees, judiciously distributing waters and forests, ponds for irrigation, and all branches of cultivation.—(U. U., ii., 94-97.)

When the human race shall have exploited the globe up to beyond the 60th degree of north latitude the temperature of the planet will be considerably milder and more regular ; the reproductive instinct will acquire greater activity ; the aurora borealis, becoming very frequent, will settle upon the pole and spread out in the form of a ring or crown. The fluid, which to-day is only luminous, will acquire a new property, that of distributing heat along with light.—(Q. M., 62.)

availing himself liberally of the poets' prerogative of lying, assures us that the fields are a dwelling-place of ineffable delights, which we know not how to RELISH ; that is the expression he uses :

> " Mais peu savent gouter leurs voluptés touchantes ;
> Pour les bien savourer c'est trop peu que des sens."

What, then, does he see so touching in the pleasure of a troop of labourers, who, exposed to the sun of the dog-days, suffer the pangs of hunger and thirst ; who, at midday, sorrily eat a crust of black bread with a glass of water, each one going off by himself, because he who has a piece of rancid bacon does not wish to share it with his neighbours ? What is there to RELISH in the sight of the privations of these poor people ? It requires Delille's name to allow such a pastoral harlequinade to pass ; and to cause the touching pleasures, which he himself recognises are but little flattering to the senses, to be *relished*.

They are no less insipid for the soul; in truth, three hundred families of a village, cultivating three hundred cabbage-patches, will find no stimulus in their labour to friendship, love, ambition, nor to the distributive passions, the tenth, eleventh, twelfth.

No COMPOSITE intrigue. In their puny, confined garden there is no charm for either the spirit or the senses. The labourer is impelled only by the sad spur of escaping famine, and providing himself with some poor cabbages, so as to sustain his famishing wife and children ; save that at night he has to watch his neighbours who will try to steal his cabbages. All these calculations are far removed from the enthusiasm demanded by the twelfth passion.

No CABALIST intrigue ; for while raising his poor cabbages, the " peasant " gives no thought to rivalries in perfection, to the choice of species, to combinations with co-operators. His sole object is to fill his poor philosophic pot, saying of the most detestable cabbages : Would to God we were always supplied with them !

No PAPILLONNE intrigue ; for, while eating his pitiful mess of cabbages, made pretty dry by lack of watering, he can have no recourse to variety of species, nor *relish* a hundred different sorts of cabbage, in the course of a year, either from his own district or from those in his vicinity ; varieties which would daily be an added bait to cultivators.

I have sufficiently demonstrated that in our civilised agriculture and manufactures, and in our rural life, everything deviates from the good and the beautiful, which have, thus far, been relegated to poetic effusions. And even the poets in their very fancies are in contradiction with associative nature ; they picture Daphnis and Chloe alongside of their tender lambs, holding crooks in their hands. Nothing in these scenes is in accordance with Nature, for, in Harmony, the shepherds and shepherdesses, leading an immense flock, are mounted upon beautiful horses and surrounded by a dozen dogs that see to it that the sheep move according to orders. The flocks, in Harmony, are always very large, their shepherds are relieved every two hours, like our sentinels, and are grouped in twos or in fours, on horseback. While in this position, they have neither crooks nor pink ribbons, nor any of those inane customs lent them by the poetry of civilisation. In these fancies, as in all the others, it has no more idea of the BEAUTIFUL in husbandry than economism has of the GOOD.

Everything concentrated or everything scattered,—that is the husbandry of civilisation : it seems to take its attorneys as its models, who, when they write by space, sometimes make their letters an inch long, and, the moment after, scrawl, when the work itself and not the number of pages is paid for. This two-fold excess is inseparable from the subversive state.—(U. U., iii., 499-501.)

The entire alimentary system of the civilised generally revolves about a single food product : wheat in Europe, rice in Asia, maize in Mexico, manioc in the Antilles.

That is the *ne plus ultra* of our policy, always *simplist* in its designs. Accordingly, we are sure of having a famine should the wheat crop not prove successful in France or Italy, or the rice crop in Hindustan or China.

Society, having started in the temperate zone, had to fix upon commodities which it produces. But when all the zones shall be cultivated, when we shall be able to calculate upon various edibles equally abundant and easy to raise in the three zones, when cultivation shall encounter no material obstacles through wars, duties, and prohibitions, or political obstacles through commercial knavery, will it be proper to make grain foods the sustaining basis of the masses? No : Harmony, which operates only by the composite principle, will create a "system of sustenance" for itself which will combine the productions of various zones.

It will make little use of bread, for three reasons :

1° Bread, a food troublesome to produce, has but little attraction for the people, who, in all countries, prefer meat and other edibles ; and, on the other hand, grain is much liked by poultry and other animals, which would be raised in immense numbers.

2° Bread is weak in industrial attraction ; all the labour connected with the production and handling of bread, such as ploughing, reaping, threshing, kneading, etc., are so little attractive that it will be necessary to add attraction by means of parochial bands, or armies of the first degree.

3° Bread, a nutriment little grateful to the taste, is, of necessity, a daily production. It will be an expensive article in Harmony, where each series will have to be allowed a compensation great in proportion as its industrial privileges are small and its labours frequent.

What edibles ought to have the preference over bread and form the chief resource of nations? It is attraction that will indicate it to us; let us consult that of different ages, and first that of children.

If we offer them the following three articles, a pound of bread, a pound of fruit, a pound of sugar, their choice will not be doubtful : they will contend for the sugar and the fruit, and disdain the bread. What are the eatables that the child desires? In the simple *régime* he likes fruit and milk foods ; and in the composite *régime* he likes these articles mixed with sugar : sweetmeats, sugared creams, and even eatables containing one-fourth of sugar, called compotes and marmalades.

Such is the diet indicated by attraction for children. And why

H

does Nature inspire them with this taste? It does so because it is expedient that man should be nourished in a bi-composite manner, combining the products of his zone and other zones, selecting those whose preparation involves little expenditure. Now, it will be seen in the special chapters, that the articles of food cited above, the compotes and marmalades, the gingerbreads and sugared creams, and, finally, the nutriment containing one-forth sugar, will, in Harmony, cost much less than bread. They will, besides, have the advantage of uniting the zones, and causing them to co-operate in the general alimentation. This method, which would be an expensive one in civilisation, is an economical one in harmony, and necessary to the general union.

Moreover, when the entire globe shall be regularly exploited, how will the enormous quantity of sugar which the torrid zone will produce be consumed, unless it be used in the popular articles of food of the temperate and *cool* zones (I do not say *frigid*, because they will be only cool after the climatic restoration)? It will be expedient then to promote the consumption of sugar, considering the facility of preserving that commodity, and the economy attaching to sugared products, some of which, such as fine confections, may be prepared a year in advance; while the labour of making bread is renewed every day, or every two or three days, according to its quality. There is no kind of good bread that can last as long as four days. That of our peasants sometimes lasts a fortnight; but the Harmonians will not eat such wretched stuff, good enough for the civilised.

In short, neither children nor adults have any great liking for bread; and as it will be more expensive than vegetables and the commodities mentioned, it will become an article of slight importance in the alimentary system of Harmony, in conformity with the desire of attraction, which is not for bread. Already the Germans and the English consume but very little of it, scarce a third of the amount eaten by the French. The variety and delicacy of the potato, combined with the low price of wines, will cause this vegetable, the preparing of which is so simple, to be quite generally preferred.

Harmony will, consequently, tend to increase greatly its herds, fowls, pasturage, orchards, gardens, and greatly reduce the vast and gloomy fields of wheat which the country now presents to us under civilisation.

As the abundance of animals will yield an enormous quantity of manure, Harmony, while cultivating only two-thirds of the ground sown with corn to-day, will reap more grain than civilisation does in double the quantity of land; for they will leave uncultivated all mediocre land, where the civilised raise sorry-looking cereals, such as those of Champagne and the environs of Paris. Such poor soil will be devoted to other uses or filled up with good earth, or joined to the forests, from which those portions suitable for cultivation will be detached.

On the other hand, Harmony does not crowd into a small stretch of territory those swarms of people that we see in China, in Bengal, in Naples, and in Würtemberg. Obliged to reserve pastures, and, above all, forests, everywhere, in order to maintain the streams and equalise the temperature, it can, even upon the best land, allow only a limited number of inhabitants, never exceeding 2,000 to the square league (20 leagues to a degree) and usually numbering 1,500 on that area.[1]

During the first century it will employ its surplus population of the various localities in peopling the colonies. After two centuries there will be no surplus, for the human species multiplies very little as soon as Harmony attains its plenitude and the race its full vigour.

In the beginning, France will be obliged, on account of lack of territory, to pour four millions of its superfluous inhabitants beyond its borders.—(U. U., iii., 567-569.)

The condition of things will, in the beginning of Harmony, favour the planting of the *vine* in semi-torrid latitudes, where spirituous wines, such as Cyprus, Madeira, Sherry, Port, Calabrian,

[1] The square league (20 leagues to a degree) represents 30 square kilometres. Fourier estimates, then, a density of population of 50 inhabitants to a square kilometre, far less, therefore, than the density of the population of France, which is even now not great enough,—about 70.—Ch. G. (*See* the chapter *De la Population.*)

Shiras, will be readily and abundantly obtained. They will serve to cross and strengthen the flat wines of France, Germany, Lombardy, and others in regions of from 40 to 50 degrees of latitude, which will be greatly improved by the climatic restoration.

Chicken-raising is evidently the branch which all the world will practise. It is in order to render this industry general that God has made the chicken the most valuable, the most wholesome of edibles, and the most generally preferred, whether for its flesh, or its eggs and the numerous uses to which these are put.— (U. U., iv., 341.)

River-fish : this edible is so much the more valuable in that it requires no care and that its excessive increase is not, like that of game, prejudicial to the crops. How great would the abundance of fish be if there were an agreement as to an intermission in fishing, and the quantity of fish to be left in every river! such an agreement is one of the properties of the associative *régime*. I have heard trustworthy experts declare that twenty times as many fish would be caught in ordinary years if an agreement could be made to fish only at the proper times, the quantity to be regulated by the requirements of reproduction, and if one-fourth of the time expended upon ruining the rivers were devoted to hunting the otter. It is thus that Association proceeds, adding to the product of the rivers that of running ponds which serve to preserve and fatten the various species.

Game : this is at once an ornament of the country, the wealth of man, and the destroyer of mischievous insects. If it is necessary to guard against the excessive multiplication of certain species, it is likewise necessary to prevent their destruction. Cultivators complain that the multitude of hunters is the cause of all crops being covered with caterpillars, since they destroy the birds that devour the grub. The hunter does not kill the sparrow, which consumes a great deal of wheat, but he kills all the birds that eat the insects and are an ornament of the country.

In speculating about an order of things in which agricultural labour would become more attractive than the chase, which consequently would be neglected, and pursued only as far as necessity demands, we shall find the following results :

Negative benefit, or increase of game without any care, nine-tenths and more.

Positive benefit, or destruction of insects.—(U. U., iii., 24-25.)

CHAPTER IX

OF MANUFACTURING PRODUCTION

THE associative order looks upon manufactures only as the complement of agriculture, a means of diversion in the passional calms which will intervene during the long winter vacation and the equatorial rains. Accordingly, all the phalanxes of the globe will have factories, but they will strive to bring the products manufactured to the highest degree of perfection, in order that their durability may reduce the labour of manufacture to a short space of time.

Let us formulate upon this subject a principle misunderstood by all economists.

God distributed only such an allowance of attraction for the work of manufacture as corresponds to a *quarter of the time* that the associative man can devote to labour. The other three quarters are to be employed in the care of animals, plants, the kitchen, industrial armies, in short, in all kinds of labour except manufacturing, in which term I do not include the daily preparation of food, for that is domestic service.

If a phalanx desired to exceed the allowance of manufacturing attraction, to carry on this species of work beyond a quarter of the time allotted to industry, in fine, to give to manufacturers half of the time at the disposal of non-domestic labour, manufacturing attraction would be found to miscarry, and, as a consequence, agricultural attraction as well ; for the agricultural series would lose a third of their time for practice, and, consequently, a third of their members : their density and activity would be found to diminish in like proportion.

Thus the entire mechanism of industrial attraction would be

perverted were they to act like the civilised, confusedly, and without maintaining the proportion of the allowance of industry to the special attractions distributed by Nature.

Moreover, this proportion would be distorted in all branches of manufacture, if, as to-day, articles were to be made of inferior quality, a thing ruinous to the social body ; for imperfect materials and dye-stuffs, by reducing the durability of a piece of clothing to a half, a third, or a fourth of what it should be, would compel a like increase in the quantity of manufactures, and restrict in the same proportion the amount of time and of hands which a population, limited to a certain fixed number, would devote to agriculture.

It is in accordance with this principle that factories, instead of being, as to-day, concentrated in cities where swarms of wretched people are huddled together, will be scattered over all the fields and phalanxes of the globe, in order that man, while applying himself to factory labour, should never deviate from the paths of attraction, which tends to make use of factories as accessories to agriculture and a change from it, not as the chief occupation, either for a district or for any of its individuals. —(N. M., 151, 153.)

PART THIRD

---•---

CHAPTER X

OF ASSOCIATION

IT has been vaguely formulated as a principle that men are made for SOCIETY : it has not been noted that society may be of two orders, the *scattered* or *disjointed* (*morcelé*) and the *combined*, the non-associative and the associative condition. The difference between the one and the other is the difference between truth and falsehood, between riches and poverty, between light and darkness, between a comet and a planet, between a butterfly and a caterpillar.

The present age, with its presentiments of association, has pursued a hesitating advance ; it has been afraid to trust to its inspirations which opened up hopes of a great discovery. It has dreamed of social union without daring to undertake the investigation of the means ; it has never thought of speculating upon the following alternative :

There can be but two methods in the exercise of industry, namely : the disjointed order or that of isolated families, such as we see, or the associative order.

God can choose for the prosecution of human labour only between GROUPS and INDIVIDUALS ; *associative and combined* action, and *incoherent and disjointed* action.

As a wise dispenser, he could not have speculated upon the employment of isolated couples, working without union, according to the civilised method ; for individual action carries within itself seven germs of disorganisation, of which each one by itself would engender a multitude of disorders. We may judge by a list of these evils whether God could for an instant have hesitated to proscribe disjointed labour which engenders them all.

EVILS OF INDIVIDUAL ACTION IN INDUSTRY.

Wage labour, indirect servitude.
1° Death of the functionary.
2° Personal inconstancy.
3° Contrast between the characters of the father and son.
4° Absence of mechanical economy.
5° Fraud, theft, and general mistrust.
6° Intermission of industry on account of lack of means.
7° Conflict of contradictory enterprises.
Opposition of individual and collective interest.
Absence of unity in plans and execution.

God would have adopted all these evils as a basis of the social system had he fixed upon the philosophic method or disjointed labour ; can we suspect the Creator of such unreason? Let us devote a little space to the examination of each of these characteristics, drawing parallels with the results of Association.

1° *Death* : it causes the cessation of a man's most useful enterprises, under circumstances in which no one about him has either the intention to continue them or the necessary talents and capital to do so.

* * The passionate Series never die : they replace every year by new neophytes the members periodically withdrawn by death.

2° *Inconstancy* : it takes possession of the individual, causes him to neglect or change the order of things ; it is opposed to the attainment of perfection and stability in the work.

* * The Series is not subject to inconstancy ; it could not cause either an intermission or versatility in its labours. If it carries off some members annually, other members enter and re-establish the equilibrium, which is, moreover, maintained by an appeal to the veterans (*anciens*), who constitute an auxiliary body in cases of urgency.

3° *Contrast between the character* of father and son, testator and heir : a contrast which causes the one to abandon or pervert the enterprises begun by the other.

* * The Series are exempt from this evil because they are formed by affinity of tastes, and not by ties of blood, which constitute a guarantee of disparity of tastes.

4° *The absence of mechanical economy*, an advantage entirely denied to individual action : it requires large masses to render all kinds of labour mechanical, whether pertaining to the household or to cultivation.

* * The Series, by the double medium of large masses and associative competition, necessarily raise mechanism to the highest degree.

5° *Fraud and theft* : evils inherent in every enterprise where the agents are not jointly interested in a distribution proportioned to the three endowments of each one — capital, labour, intelligence.

* * The serial mechanism, entirely safe from fraud and theft, is exempted from the ruinous precautions which these two dangers demand.

6° *The intermission of industry* : lack of work, land, machinery, implements, workshops, and other gaps which constantly paralyse civilised industry.

* * These impediments are unknown in the associative *régime*, which is always and abundantly provided with everything that is necessary for the perfection and the continuity of labour.

7° *Conflicting enterprises* : civilised rivalries are malevolent, not emulative ; a manufacturer strives to crush his competitor : the workmen are the respective opposing legions.

* * Nothing of this unsocial spirit in the Series, each one of which is interested in the success of the others, and which undertake only such labour, whether in the field or in the factory, as is guaranteed a market.

8° *Opposition of the two kinds of interest, individual and collective*, as in the destruction of forests, the game, fisheries, and the debasement of climatic conditions.

* * Opposite effect of the Series : general agreement for the maintenance of the sources of wealth, and the restoration of climatic conditions in the integral composite manner.

9° Finally, *wage labour, or indirect servitude*, guarantee of misfortune, of persecution, of despair, for the workman in civilisation or barbarism.

* * Striking contrast to the lot of the associative workman, who is in full enjoyment of the nine natural definite rights.

After perusing this table, everyone can arrive at a conclusion, and recognise that God, having had the option of these two kinds of mechanism, of an ocean of absurdities and an ocean of perfection, could not even have deliberated about his choice.

Any hesitation would have formed a contradiction to his characteristics, notably to that of *economy of means* : he would have acted in opposition to it in choosing the disjointed order and proscribing Association, which effects every species of economy : saving coercion, stagnation, health, time, *ennui*, hand-labour, machinery, contrivances, uncertainties, knavery, preventives, waste, and duplicity of action.

All the sophists agree in declaring that *man is made for society* : according to this principle ought man to aim for the smallest or the largest society possible ? It is beyond doubt that it is in the largest that all the mechanical and economical advantages will be found : and since we have only attained the infinitely small, "family-labour" ("*travail familial*"), is any other indication required to verify the fact that civilisation is the antipodes of destiny as well as of truth ?—(U. U., iv., 126, 128.)

Short-sighted politicians, who thought they were making wise tests when they experimented with small aggregations of about twenty families, fell into the double error :

1° *Of making attempts with a small number, which yields neither large economies nor the resources of mechanism.*

2° *Of making the family-spirit the spring of action ; a spirit, which, tending to egoism, ought to be absorbed in corporate union.*

1st Mistake. Induction from the small to the great: it is doubtless quite impossible to unite 2, 3, 4 households, and even 10 to 12; the conclusion has therefore been drawn that it would be so much the more impossible to unite 2 to 300 of them.

In this view of the case, the moderns may be compared to timid navigators, like those who, before Christopher Columbus, did not dare advance beyond 200, 300, 400 leagues upon the Atlantic; each one returned full of consternation, declaring that that ocean was a boundless abyss, and that it was folly to venture upon it. Had a more daring spirit pushed out 600 or 800 leagues without discovering America, everybody would most complacently have concluded that the hypothesis of a new continent was an absurdity. Finally, if a vessel, still bolder, had pushed out 1,000 or 1,200 leagues, it would likewise have returned unsuccessful, and everyone would so much the more have classed the attempt in the rank of follies; yet, in order to succeed, it was only necessary to persist and advance 1,800 leagues.

Such is the method that should have been followed in the study of Association. The only effort required of genius was to persist in advancing, not to be discouraged by experiments on a small scale, not to conclude from the small to the great, but to keep on with experiments on a gradually ascending scale. If an experiment with 4 families proved a failure, it should have been tried with 8; 8 proving a failure, with 16; if 16 miscarried, with 32, then with 64, then with 100. Having reached that point, they would have succeeded provided they had discovered the methods of the passionate Series and short sessions, which are easily found if the experiments are made with 350 to 400 persons. Had these experiments been pursued for half a century, the discovery would necessarily have been made of the mechanism of the series, which will be described in this work.—(U. U., iii., 508.)

The bodies of colonists which are often formed in Europe, and which emigrate to America or the Crimea, would not be suitable for an experiment of even minimum association, termed *sous-*

hongrée. The mechanism of the series requires a graduated variety of age, fortune, character, knowledge, etc. The low grade No. 1 is the least exacting as regards this variety, but yet it requires some gradation, and that is what is lacking in these assemblages of emigrants for the colonies : they consist of people for the most part without means ; they frequently have no old people or children ; they lack many other indispensable features. However, if one of these assemblages were chosen as a nucleus, it would be easy to add the variety required for the low grade of 400 persons.

It would not, then, suffice to combine a certain number of people ; it is necessary, besides, to assort them according to graduated inequalities of every property, and to extend the scale of inequality in proportion to the degree of the experiment ; that is to say, that in the high degree the scale of gradation should range from the man without any means, grade 0, up to the man owning a hundred millions ; while in the low degree a scale of small graduated fortunes, 0 to 20,000 francs of capital, will be sufficient.—(U. U., iii., 439.)

Various sophists, doubtless well-intentioned, have within recent years published some writings upon an inferior branch of association.

They have all been mistaken, beginning with the title ; for they have taken for the chief social bond an inconsiderable subdivision which leads only to the farming-out and monopoly of great industries,—a bond which ought to be denominated *share-holding concentration.*

Share-holding concentration unites the heads and not the co-operators ; it is an arrangement, specious enough, which starts out brilliantly and recommends itself by great and useful enterprises ; such are, in the material world, the Caledonian Canal ; in the political, the English East India Company.

But whither does such action tend ? what would its influence be when, once become general, it should have invaded and delivered over to joint-stock companies all branches of industry ? I say ALL, because if these companies are as yet ignorant of the means of reducing agriculture to a monopoly through contractors and sub-contractors, they will very soon discover those means ; *l'appetit vient en mangeant ;* then, taking advantage of a moment of war and distress, they will persuade the Government to grant them the concession.

Then would be organised a federation of graduated and affiliated monopolies,—the advent of commercial feudalism, or the fourth phase of civilised progress.

Civilisation began with leagues of vassals or oligarchs, noble or patriarchal ; it is destined to end with the return of great vassals of a different species, the merchants or heads of joint stock companies. The meeting of extremes is a general law of motion, a law which is reproduced in all material phenomena, as, for instance, in the phases of the moon, which, beginning with a direct crescent, ends with an inverse crescent.

If for *shareholding-concentration* the title of association is claimed, it is taking the form for the substance, since the substance embraces two primordial functions : agricultural and domestic administration, to which our present writers have devoted no attention. They understand how to join only the upper links, the heads. In association they have grasped the shadow, not the reality.

Despite this error, the sophists whom I refute are none the less praiseworthy for their efforts. All science begins with groping, partial successes, leading by degrees to an unequal solution of problems. Now, this groping, which I have described under the name of *concentration,* is more laudable than the apathy of the preceding ages regarding the most urgent of questions.—(U. U., i., Preface 96, 97.)

We see in the civilised *régime* gleams of association, *merely material,* germs due to instinct and not to science. Instinct teaches the hundred families of a village that a common oven will involve much less expenditure in masonry and fuel than a hundred small household ovens, and that it will be better managed by two or three practised bakers than the hundred small ovens by a hundred women, who will, twice out of three times, fail to secure the proper degree of heat for the oven and the proper baking of the bread.

Good sense has taught the inhabitants of the north that if each family desired to produce its own beer, it would be more expensive than good wines. A domestic union, a military mess, comprehend instinctively that a single kitchen, cooking for thirty guests, will be better and less costly than twenty separate kitchens.

The peasants of the Jura, seeing that a certain cheese, called *Gruyère*, could not be prepared from the milk of a single household, combine together, take their milk daily to a common work-house, where an account is kept of each one's contribution, noted in figures upon pieces of wood ; and from the aggregation of these small quantities of milk, they produce, at slight expense, a great cheese in a huge kettle.—(N. M., 7.)

A presentiment of the discovery of industrial association has for some time existed in England, which is instituting active researches and costly experiments in the organisation of domestic association. The English, confused by beholding, the same as everywhere else, the wretchedness of the masses increase in proportion to the national wealth and the advance in industry, must have thought that it required some new method to emerge from this labyrinth. They rightly presumed that associative industry would afford expedients whereby the lot of the lower classes would be ameliorated ; their attempts have not proved fortunate ; this failure ought not to astonish them : association was a virgin field, a new scientific world, where one must needs go astray without the guide of theory or compass.

According to the details furnished by the journalists of the English establishments confided to the direction of Mr. Owen, it appears that three capital errors have been committed there, of which each one independently would have been sufficient to cause the failure of the undertaking ; let us analyse these errors.

1° *Excess of numbers.* There are, it is said, 500 or 600 families engaged in these attempts, say 3,000 individuals. That is far too many, for the highest degree of association admits only

16,000 to 17,000 persons, men, women, and children, and the lowest degree may be limited to 400.

2° *Equality.* This is a political poison in association ; the English are ignorant of that fact, and constitute their commuities of families of about equal fortune. The associative *régime* is as incompatible with equality of fortune as with uniformity of character ; it desires a progressive scale in every direction, the greatest variety in employments, and, above all, the union of extreme contrasts, such as that of the man of opulence with one of no means, a fiery character with an apathetic one, youth with age, etc.

3° *The absence of agriculture.* It is impossible to organise a regular and well-balanced association without bringing into play the labours of the field, or at least gardens, orchards, flocks and herds, poultry-yards, and a great variety of species, animal and vegetable. They are ignorant of this principle in England, where they experiment with artisans, with manufacturing labour alone, which cannot by itself suffice to sustain social union. Factories are requisite in the three modes of association, but they are interposed only as stages between agricultural labours, which are the mainstay of industrial rivalries and intrigues.

Chief error : the head denies himself all share in the profits ; he lacks the motive of interest.

A statement of these errors is sufficient to establish the fact that the moderns have been very far from the discovery of the principles of association.—(U. U., ii., 35.)

Owen's scheme of communism had some vogue at first, because it was a mask for party spirit, a veil to cover the secret plan which tends to destroy the clergy and religion. That perspective caused the whole *coterie* of atheism to rally round the preacher Owen. As for his other two dogmas, that of community of goods is so pitiful that it is not worthy of refutation ; that of the sudden abolishment of marriage is also a monstrosity.

Genuine association will pursue the three opposite courses : 1° It will be religious through inclination, through conviction of the exalted wisdom of God, whose benefits it will enjoy every moment.

Public worship will be a necessity for it : the most insignificant vicar will be as well placed as the bishops of to-day, and it will be necessary to create at least thirty thousand priests in France by hasty ordination, in order that each phalanx may contain a sufficient number to allow them to discharge their duties in relays, not subjecting them to a daily exercise of their functions ; 2° in opposition to the spirit of communism, the spirit of ownership will be aroused by labour-coupons and economic votes, accorded to the proletarians who shall, by assiduous economy, have accumulated one-twelfth of the capital entitling one to a vote in the areopagus : such votes will be granted for many other reasons as well, so as to avoid imitating the civilised, who, in their system of representation, estimate merit only by the token of money ; 3° as regards marriage, it has been seen that it will *with time* be modified, graduated, and not suppressed ; and the question will only be agitated by degrees in the succeeding generation, when the modifications shall have been voted by four combined classes : government, the clergy, fathers, and husbands.

However, it is a proof of the intellectual convulsion of the age that it has allowed itself to be deluded in regard to the most important problem of the social world, in regard to the associative mechanism, by a preacher who has neither new doctrines nor distinct dogmas. His scheme of destruction of the clergy is a residue of revolution : if all the classes that abused their functions were to be abolished, I know not what class among the civilised could be maintained. His dogma of communism is a rehash of Sparta and Rome ; that of free love is likewise a plagiarism from various peoples, among others the Nepaulians, the Otaheitans, etc. —(N. M., 473.)

To sum up, all our reformers feel and proclaim the necessity of uniting the working classes into masses or social phalanxes, but they do not wish to acknowledge that the associative process belongs to a science of which the economists have no conception, and of which I alone have formulated a regular theory, ample and without gaps, attacking and solving all problems, boldly presenting those before which all economists have recoiled, such as the equilibrium of population, industry attractive and guaranteeing the good morals of the people.[1]—(F. I., 9.)

[1] The Jesuits of Paraguay had given to association (forced, equivocal) quite a great development : but everything that is based upon coercion is fragile and denotes the absence of genius.—(Manuscrits, p. 66.)

CHAPTER XI

THE COMMUNAL COUNTING-HOUSE

MERCHANTS are occupied solely with crushing each other: such is the effect of free competition. It is necessary that agriculture, *crushed* by their underhand dealings, should resort to the freedom enjoyed by commerce and crush them in its turn, by an undertaking which I shall designate as the *joint-stock communal counting-house*, an establishment serving the purposes of commerce and agricultural management, acting as a depository, and advancing money to the consigner. The said counting-house calculated for sub-divisions consisting of at least 1,500 people, would be provided with a garden, loft, cellar, kitchen, and communal factories—two at the least.

How ought such establishments to be organised? That is a question I shall not enter into here, where I merely wish to point out the chief advantages of the joint-stock communal counting-house, which, among other properties, would possess those of:

Reducing by half the domestic administration of poor and even medium households;

Paying upon a certain fixed day, in advance and without involving expense, the taxes of the community;

Advancing money at the lowest market rate to every agriculturist whose estate presented a guarantee;

Furnishing each individual with every commodity, indigenous or foreign, at the lowest rates, by freeing him from the intermediary profits obtained by merchants and jobbers;

Securing profitable employment at all seasons (of the year) to the indigent class; varied occupations, without excess or subordination of either field or factory labour.

There has been a foreshadowing of the establishment in question, communal Guaranteeism, both in a *general* and in a *partial sense :*

Experiment in the general sense : it was a feeling of the necessity of assisting the poor of the country districts that occasioned the reservation of woods and pasture-lands, under the name of *commons,* designed both for the poor and the rich.   It is admitted that the arrangement is a mistaken one, that the poor devastate the commons, and that they are miserably managed.   In this enterprise for general usefulness, then, the means employed for helping the poor have proved a failure.

The *partial* attempts have been even greater failures, such as the district banks and other companies, which, pretending to assist agriculture and the small proprietor, have been convicted of vexatious usury, of lending at a yearly interest of 17 per cent. Present-day genius is only prolific of this species of inventions.

These different forms of assistance and a hundred others would be provided by the joint-stock communal counting-house.   Let us imagine it organised, without lingering over the details of its arrangement.   It is a vast establishment which saves the poor man every kind of petty labour.   This poor man is the owner of a small field and a small vineyard ; but how can he have a good loft, a good cellar, good casks, adequate implements and contrivances ?   He finds all these in the communal counting-house ; he may, after an agreement as to terms, deposit his grain and his wine there, and receive an advance of two-thirds of their supposed value.   That is all that would be desired by the peasant, always compelled to sell at a very low rate at harvest-time.   He would not dread paying interest upon an advance ; he always pays 12 per cent. interest for an advance to the usurers ; he will bless the counting-house which will advance him money at 6 per cent. a year—the commercial rate—and save him the expenses of management; for a small farmer will be paid at the counting-house, without furnishing the contrivances for doing a work which he would have done gratuitously in his own place, with the added expense of those contrivances.   In point of fact :

He has consigned his crop—twenty quintals of wheat and two hogsheads of wine—to the counting-house; it is not he who furnishes the sacks, the casks, and the waggons and animals used to convey them to the market; his harvest reaped and stored, he works by the day for the counting-house, and is paid, while at the same time he is attending to his wheat and his wine, which are being raised in value, for they are added to a mass of grain, a tun of wine of the same quality. He may even be saved the trouble of fermentation, and have his vintage accepted according to the customary valuation.

The labour required to protect the grain from rats and beetles, and to manipulate four or five tons, amounts to about one-tenth of that which would be entailed in a great number of petty households, the poorest of which will be casually employed by the counting-house in its granaries, cellars, gardens, and workshops. They cannot at any time lack work there, and the benefit they derive by consigning to the counting-house is so much the more considerable in that it allows them ample time for rest, through saving of manipulation and even of cooking, for, upon consigning any commodities, they draw upon the communal kitchen for a certain quantity of provisions, imitating our small households, which, in order to economise, get their meals from a restaurant.

The counting-house lays in a supply of all such articles as are sure of a demand; ordinary stuffs, commodities of primary necessity, and drugs in general use. By procuring them from their sources, it is able to furnish them to the consigners at a small profit, to show them the accounts of the purchase and costs. These advantages constitute so many attractions for consigning. If the counting-house is well managed it ought in less than three years to be metamorphosed into semi-association; for it will be sought by the rich as well as the poor; every rich person will seek the advantage of being a voting shareholder in it; the small non-shareholding consigner will, in the sittings of the Exchange, have a consulting voice as to the chances of sale; the shareholder will vote on the sales and purchases.

Nothing pleases a countryman, and particularly a peasant, more than assemblies of commercial intrigue. That is an attraction which he would enjoy weekly at the communal counting-house where he would gather intelligence of commercial correspondence, and where would be debated the expediency of sales and purchases. The peasant, though little disposed to illusions, would eagerly covet the vainglory of the shareholder debating sales and purchases in the communal counting-house, or at least the rank of consigner with a consulting voice. Peasants form an *exchange* every Sunday ; at the church entrance, before or after high mass ; they form an exchange in the markets and taverns, where they exhaust themselves with inquiries and prattle, about the state of affairs, about the rise and decline in commodities : they would, at the counting-house, have a genuine exchange, and be eager, in order to figure there, to become shareholders, or consigners, or both.

It would have been very fitting to inaugurate such establishments in the small market-towns which contain an unoccupied monastery. It could easily have been adapted to the uses of the communal counting-house, particularly as the monks paid great attention to the construction of their lofts and cellars, had extensive gardens,—a necessary requirement of the establishments in question,—and huge halls well suited for reunions, and for " three " factories. The counting-house must be provided with the latter, in order to furnish varied occupation in winter as well as in summer to the poorer class, and not disgust them with labour by the uniformity which prevails in our public and private workshops,—a monotony in direct opposition to the designs of Nature, which demands variety in industry as in all other things.

The communal counting-house would, in its organisation, resemble Harmonist methods as closely as possible : it could have fields and flocks, in proportion to its means, at its service ; and it would always give its employees, even the poorest of them, a part interest in some special products, such as wool, fruits, vegetables, etc., in order to awaken in them that activity, that industrial solicitude, which is generated by associative participation, and to preserve them from the indifference which characterises civilised wage-earners.

Such an enterprise should have been the first to engross the attention of societies devoted to the maintenance of agricultural industry.—(U. U., iii., 281-285.)

The most conspicuous advantage would be the downfall of commerce. All the repositories (*fermes d'asile*) would co-operate, through the medium of the minister and the prefects, to do without merchants, to carry on their buying and selling directly with each other; they would have an abundance of commodities for sale, because they would have storehouses where the small cultivators or proprietors who have neither good lofts nor good cellars, nor a quantity of servants, would gladly deposit their products, paying a moderate charge for storage and sale. Besides, the owner would, on depositing in these storehouses, receive an advance at a moderate rate of interest, and thereby be relieved from premature sales, which cause the debasement of commodities.

Henceforth all the friends of commerce, the hosts of merchants, would find themselves stranded, like a string of spiders that perish in their web for lack of insects when it is shut up so tight that it precludes admission. This downfall of the merchants would be the result of *free competition*, for they would not be prevented from trading; but nobody would have confidence in them, because the repositories and their provincial agencies would offer adequate guarantees of truth.—(N. M., 433.)

By building upon this foundation there could already be erected an edifice of semi-happiness, or GUARANTEEISM, a period between the civilised state and the associative state.

Semi-association is collective without being individual; withou joining lands or households in a combined management. It admits the isolated labour of families; but it establishes a solidarity or comparative assurance among them extending over the *entire* mass, so that no individual may be excepted from the benefits of the guarantees.

The counting-house referred to, among its other undertakings, would have a pharmacy, where it would make an honest profit, while, at the same time, rendering valuable services to the villagers.

The same would be the case with a hundred other social benefits, upon which time is wasted in vain dreams : they can only be the fruit of associative methods, and not of unassociated labour. Now, the first, the smallest germ of agricultural association is the communal counting-house—initiative and sketch of social union, quickest road for entering upon guaranteeism, or the sixth period. That, therefore, was the inquiry which should have engaged the attention of students who profess to attain social guarantees without abandoning disjointed labour and incoherent management :—where shall we find students willing to devote their vigils to useful inventions, when it is so easy to acquire fame by sophistry !—(U. U., iii., 296.)

CHAPTER XII

THE PHALANSTERY

THE announcement does, I acknowledge, sound very improbable, of a method for combining three hundred families unequal in fortune, and rewarding each person,—man, woman, child— according to the three properties, *capital, labour, talent.* More than one reader will credit himself with humour when he remarks: "Let the author try to associate but three families, to reconcile three households in the same dwelling to social union, to arrangements of purchases and expenses, to perfect harmony in passions, character, and authority; when he shall have succeeded in reconciling three mistresses of associated households, we shall believe that he can succeed with thirty and with three hundred."

I have already replied to an argument which it is well to reproduce (for repetition will frequently be necessary here); I have observed *that as economy can spring only from large combinations, God had to create a social theory applicable to large masses and not to three or four families.*

An objection seemingly more reasonable, and which needs to be refuted more than once, is that of social discords. How conciliate the passions, the conflicting interests, the incompatible characters,—in short, the innumerable disparities which engender so much discord?

It may easily have been surmised that I shall make use of a lever entirely unknown, and whose properties cannot be judged until I shall have explained them. The passional contrasted Series draws its nourishment solely from those disparities which bewilder civilised policy; it acts like the husbandman who from a mass of filth draws the germs of abundance ; the refuse, the dirt, and impure matter which would serve only to defile and infect our dwellings, are for him the sources of wealth.—(U. U., ii., 29.)

If social experiments have miscarried, it is because some fatality has impelled all speculators to work with bodies of poor people whom they subjected to a *monastic-industrial* discipline, chief obstacle to the working of the series. Here, as in everything else, it is ever SIMPLISM (*simplisme*) which misleads the civilised, obstinately sticking to experiments with combinations of the poor ; they cannot elevate themselves to the conception of a trial with combinations of the rich. They are veritable Lemning rats (migrating rats of Lapland), preferring drowning in a pond to deviating from the route which they have decided upon.[1] — (U. U., iii., 156.)

It is necessary for a company of 1,500 to 1,600 persons to have a stretch of land comprising a good square league, say a surface of six million square *toises* (do not let us forget that a third of that would suffice for the simple mode).[2]

[1] It has been urged that I made an experiment at Condé S. V., and *that it did not succeed ;* that, too, is one of the calumnies of pandemonium. I did nothing at Condé ; an architect, who held sway there, was not willing to allow any part of my plan. His was a spirit of contradiction, repelling everything that did not proceed from himself ; a rabid Anglomaniac, who would have nothing but what he had seen in England, or rather, his fancies, which varied from one day to the next.

In vain did I represent to him that he could not in England have seen buildings arranged for industry carried on by series of groups, for none such are to be found there ; he took no notice of that, and, after changing his plans ten times and shifting his landmarks as often, he began by constructing a *provisional rhapsody* upon swampy ground below the level of the water. I could not agree to this absurd method of building, which would not have been of any use in combined industry, and which only served to disgust visitors, to prevent them from taking shares, and to give the propitious moment of favour the slip. I severed my connection with the affair, had nothing further to do with it, not wishing to compromise myself by appearing to co-operate in arrangements which served no purpose for the associative mechanism.— (F. I., 5.)

[2] I had promised a very detailed article upon approximations to the associative mechanism : Companies with slender means might wish to start on a small scale ; that is the favourite method of the French,—to outline, to grope. The greater number would advocate a trial reduced to a half, to 900 persons, or to a third, 600 persons.

The land should be provided with a fine stream of water; it should be intersected by hills, and adapted to varied cultivation; it should be contiguous to a forest, and not far removed from a large city, but sufficiently so to escape intruders.

The experimental Phalanx standing alone, and without the support of neighbouring phalanxes, will, in consequence of this isolation, have so many gaps in attraction, and so many passional calms to dread in its workings, that it will be necessary to provide it with the aid of a good location fitted for a variety of functions. A flat country such as Antwerp, Leipsic, Orleans, would be totally unsuitable, and would cause many Series to fail, owing to the uniformity of the land surface. It will, therefore, be necessary to select a diversified region, like the surroundings of Lausanne, or, at the very least, a fine valley provided with a stream of water and a forest, like the valley of Brussels or of Halle. A fine location near Paris would be the stretch of country lying between Poissy and Confleurs, Poissy and Meulan.

A company will be collected consisting of from 1,500 to 1,600 persons of graduated degrees of fortune, age, character, of theoretical and practical knowledge; care will be taken to secure the greatest amount of variety possible, for the greater the number of variations either in the passions or the faculties of the members, the easier will it be to make them harmonise in a short space of time.

In this district devoted to experiment, there ought to be combined every species of practicable cultivation, including that in conservatories and hot-houses; in addition, there ought to be at least three accessory factories, to be used in winter and on rainy

---

I call their attention to the fact that in reducing a mechanism, its system is perverted, unless all the parts are retained : we can reduce a huge belfry-clock to proportions small enough to be enclosed in a minute case, to a watch an inch in diameter ; but this watch contains all the parts of the large mechanism, even the arrangement for striking; hence, the system, though reduced, is not changed.

It is not so with a mechanism of the passions : in order to reduce it in the same proportion as the cathedral clock to a little watch, we should have to have miniature people, Liliputians half a foot high, and animals and vegetables of proportionate dimensions.—(N. M., 380.)

days ; furthermore, various practical branches of science and the arts, independent of the schools.

Above all, it will be necessary to fix the valuation of the capital invested in shares ; lands, materials, flocks, implements, etc. This point ought, it seems, to be among the first to receive attention ; I think it best to dismiss it here. I shall limit myself to remarking that all these investments in transferable shares and stock-coupons will be represented.

A great difficulty to be overcome in the experimental Phalanx will be the formation of the ties of high mechanism or collective bonds of the Series, before the close of the first season. It will be necessary to accomplish the passional union of the mass of the members ; to lead them to collective and individual devotion to the maintenance of the Phalanx, and, especially, to perfect harmony regarding the division of the profits, according to the three factors, *Capital, Labour, Talent.*

This difficulty will be greater in northern than in southern countries, owing to the difference between devoting eight months and five months to agricultural labour.

An experimental Phalanx, being obliged to start out with agricultural labour, will not be in full operation until the month of May (in a climate of 50 degrees, say in the region around London or Paris) ; and, since it will be necessary to form the bonds of general union, the harmonious ties of the Series, before the suspension of field labour, before the month of October, there will be barely five months of full practice in a region of 50 degrees : the work will have to be accomplished in that short space.

The trial would, therefore, be much more conveniently made in a temperate region, like Florence, Naples, Valencia, Lisbon,[1]

[1] Nature supplies every globe with a focus, or central seat of government. Our focus is Constantinople, a locality favoured with every species of perfection.

Mouth of a great and splendid salt-water river, which bears vessels of the largest size, and which, issuing from a sea, forms neither alluvia nor deltas.

1° Gigantic harbour, as convenient as it is magnificent.

2° Small fresh-water river, very pure, situated at the head of the harbour, and adequate for the required supply.

where they would have eight to nine months of full cultivation and a far better opportunity to consolidate the bonds of union, since there would be but two or three months of passional calm remaining to tide over till the advent of the second spring, a time when the Phalanx, resuming agricultural labour, would form its ties and cabals anew with much greater zeal, imbuing them with a degree of intensity far above that of the first year; it would thenceforth be in a state of complete consolidation, and strong enough to weather the passional calm of the second winter.

We shall see in the chapter on hiatuses of attraction, that the first Phalanx will, in consequence of its social isolation and other impediments inherent to the experimental canton, have twelve special obstacles to overcome, obstacles which the Phalanxes subsequently founded would not have to contend with. That is why it is so important that the experimental canton should have the assistance coming from field-work prolonged eight or nine months, like that in Naples and Lisbon.—(U. U., iii., 427, 429.)

As for the selection to be made among the candidates, rich and poor, various qualities which are accounted vicious or useless in civilisation should be looked for ; such are :

A good ear for music.
Good manners of families.
Aptitude for the fine arts.

3° Purifying eddy, skirting, sweeping the harbour, and carrying off the surplus of fresh water.
4° Situation, semi-central in the great continent, and accessible by sea from the small one.
5° Locality within reach of the products of all zones.
6° Meeting-point for all lines of communication by sea and land.
7° Surpassing beauty of its diversified sites, and of the view, both near and distant.
The most propitious and the most grateful climate, after correction of the temperature by general cultivation and transformation of the noxious winds of the Black Sea, caused by the uncultivated condition of the east and the north.
Favoured with so many advantages, that site will be selected for the capital of the globe, with the advent of the third generation of Harmony; after the time required to rebuild the city, and divide it among urban phalanxes, that will not tolerate our unwholesome dwellings.—(F. I., 8.)

And various rules which are contrary to philosophic ideas should be followed.

> To prefer families having few children.
> To have one-third of the organisation consist of celibates.
> To seek characters regarded as peculiar.
> To establish a graduated scale respecting age, fortune, knowledge.

In view of the necessity of uniform education and fusion of the classes among children, I have advised, what I now reiterate, the selection, for the experimental Phalanx, of well-bred families, particularly in the lower class, since it will be necessary to have that class mingle in labour with the rich, and to make the latter find a charm in this amalgamation. That charm will be greatly dependent upon the good breeding of the inferiors ; that is why the people in the environs of Paris, Blois, and Tours will be very suitable for the trial, provided, of course, that a proper selection is made.—(N. M., 104, 178.)

Let us proceed with the details of composition.

At least seven-eighths of the members ought to be cultivators and manufacturers ; the remainder will consist of capitalists, scholars, and artists.

The Phalanx would be badly graded and difficult to balance, if among its capitalists there were several having 100,000 francs, several 50,000 francs, without intermediate fortunes. In such a case it would be necessary to seek to procure intermediate fortunes of 60,000, 70,000, 80,000, 90,000 francs. The Phalanx best graduated in every respect raises social harmony and profits to the highest degree.—(U. U., iii., 431.)

One is tempted to believe that our sybarites would not wish to be associated with Grosjean and Margot : they are so even now (as I believe I have already pointed out). Is not the rich man obliged to discuss his affairs with twenty peasants who occupy his farms, and who are all agreed in taking illegal advantage of him ? He is, therefore, *the peasant's associate*, obliged to make inquiries about the good and the bad farmers, their character, morals, solvency, and industry ; *he does associate in a very direct and a very tiresome way* with Grosjean and Margot. In Harmony, he will be their indirect associate, being relieved of accounts regarding the management, which will be regulated by the regents, proctors, and special officers, without its being necessary for the capitalist to intervene or to run any risk of fraud. He will, therefore, be freed from the disagreeable features of his present association with the peasantry ; he will form a new one, where he will not furnish them anything, and where they will only be his obliging and devoted friends, in accordance with the details given regarding the management of the Series and of reunions. If he takes the lead at festivals, it is because he has agreed to accept the rank of captain. If he gives them a feast, it is because he takes pleasure in acknowledging their continual kind attentions.

Thus the argument urged about the repugnance to association between Mondor and Grosjean, *already associated in fact*, is only, like all the others, a quibble devoid of sense.—(U. U., iv., 518.

The edifice occupied by a Phalanx does not in any way resemble our constructions, whether of the city or country ; and none of our buildings could be used to establish a large Harmony of 1,600 persons,—not even a great palace like Versailles, nor a great monastery like the Escurial. If, for the purposes of experiment, only an inconsiderable Harmony of 200 or 300 members, or a *hongrée* of 400 members is organised, a monastery or a palace (Meudon) could be used for it.

The lodgings, plantations, and stables of a Society conducted on the plan of Series of groups, must differ vastly from our villages and country towns, which are intended for families having no social connection, and which act in a perverse manner ; in place of that class of little houses which rival each other in filth and ungainliness in our little towns,[1] a Phalanx constructs an

---

[1] The principle of SIMPLE OWNERSHIP *is the right of arbitrarily obstructing the general good, in order to gratify individual fancies.* Accordingly, we see full liberty granted to the vandals who follow their fancy for compromising healthfulness and beauty by erecting grotesque constructions, caricatures, which are sometimes more costly than handsome, good buildings. These

edifice for itself which is as regular as the ground permits : here is a sketch of distribution for a location favourable to development.

The central part of the Palace or Phalanstery ought to be appropriated to peaceful uses, and contain the dining-halls, halls for finance, libraries, study, etc. In this central portion are located the place of worship, the *tour d'ordre*, the telegraph, the post-office boxes, the chimes for ceremonials, the observatory, the winter court adorned with resinous plants, and situated in the rear of the parade-court.

One of the wings ought to combine all the noisy workshops, such as the carpenter-shop, the forge, all hammer-work ; it ought to contain also all the industrial gatherings of children, who are generally very noisy in industry and even in music. This combination will obviate a great annoyance of our civilised cities, where we find some man working with a hammer in every street, some dealer in iron or tyro on the clarionet, who shatter the tympanum of fifty families in the vicinity.

The other wing ought to contain the caravansary with its ball-rooms and its halls appropriated to intercourse with outsiders, so that these may not encumber the central portion of the palace and embarrass the domestic relations of the Phalanx.—(U. U., iii., 447, 455.)

The Phalanstery, or edifice of the experimental Phalanx, ought to be constructed of inexpensive material,—wood, brick, etc., because, I repeat, it would be impossible in that first attempt to determine precisely the dimensions suitable either for each individual seristery, the portion designed for the public relations of the series, or for the various workshops, storerooms, stables, etc.

An indication of the wrong spirit and impotence which prevail

vandals, with a cruel avarice, frequently build unwholesome, wretchedly ventilated houses, into which they economically huddle a swarm of people ; and these murderous speculations are dignified with the name of liberty. It were as well to license the quacks, who, abusing the credulity of the people, practise medicine without possessing any knowledge. They also can say that they are turning their industry to account, that they are availing themselves of *imprescriptible rights.*—(U. U., iii., 309.)

in this respect, is the fact that there is no law bearing upon RELATIVE OBLIGATIONS, as regards healthfulness and beauty. For instance, if a city buys and demolishes a collection of hovels which obstructed four streets, it is certain that the houses on the four sides adjacent to this collection will greatly rise in value ; there will be a better circulation of air ; instead of having an ugly mask opposite their façades, they will have a place ornamented with trees and fountains ; they will, therefore, have gained considerably by this demolition, and increased their rents in proportion. They owe, in all fairness, a share in the resulting profit to the community which has, with its money, procured them this increase of the useful and the agreeable, this transition from the ill to the good. Nevertheless, no law compels them to indemnify it by relinquishing half of their profits. Far from it ; the owner favoured by this improvement will not bequeath a groat to the community that has enriched him, and if it asks him for some subsidy, some share in the profits, be it but a fourth, he will answer ironically : "I did not request you to demolish the houses which masked mine ; I do not owe you any indemnity for your outlay in improvements."—(U. U., iii., 309, 310.)

In civilisation the idea has never been considered of perfecting that part of our raiment which is called the atmosphere, with which we are in perpetual contact. It is not sufficient to modify it in the *salons* of some people of leisure, who, themselves, will take cold in going from their houses into the midst of the fog. The atmosphere must be modified by a general system adapted to all the functions of the human race ; and this correction ought to be COMPOSITE, affecting that which is *essential*, or the general gradation of climates, and that which is *accessory*, or local gradation, which they do not even know of in our capitals ; for we see in Paris an open Bazaar, called the *Palais Royal*, whose covered galleries are neither heated in winter nor ventilated in summer. It is the superlative of poverty, compared to the associative state, in which the poorest man will have heated and ventilated passage-ways, tents and shelters for all his functions ; outside of a small class of public services, such as the post, which must be carried on in the open air, whatever the temperature; but the exception of an eighth proves the rule. Besides, services of this sort will be consigned to individuals whose temperament can accommodate itself to it, and who will look upon it as play, considering the large profits obtained.—(U. U., iii., 37.)

The most poverty-stricken of the Harmonians, a man who hasn't a farthing, gets into a vehicle in a portico well heated and inclosed; he goes from the Palace to the stables through paved and gravelled underground passages; he passes from his dwelling to the public halls and the workshops through galleried streets which are heated in winter and ventilated in summer. In Harmony one can pass through the workshops, stables, shops, ball-rooms, banquet and assembly-halls, etc., in January, without knowing whether it is rainy or windy, hot or cold; and the details which I shall give upon this subject authorise me to say that if the civilised after 3000 years of research have not yet learned how to house themselves, it is little surprising that they have not yet learned to direct and harmonise their passions. When one fails in the pettiest material calculations, one may well fail in the great calculations concerning the passions.

This sheltered communication is all the more necessary in Harmony in that the changes there are very frequent, the sessions of the groups never lasting more than an hour or two. If the Harmonians were obliged, in crossing from one hall to another, from a stable to a workshop, to pass through the open air, the result would be that they would, in a week of rigorous wintry weather or fogs, be riddled with colds, inflammations, pleurisy, no matter how robust their constitution. A state of things which necessitates frequent changes imperatively demands sheltered means of communication; and that is one of the reasons why it will be very difficult to organise in a great monastery even the smallest of Harmonies, the minimum degree K., although that would be composed of the lower classes, quite inured to the rigours of the atmosphere.

The galleried street, or continued Peristyle, is located in the second story. It is not adaptable to the ground floor, which must have openings at various points to admit of archways for vehicles.

Those who have seen the gallery of the Louvre, or *Musée de Paris*, may consider it as a model of the galleried street of Harmony—which will likewise have a floor and be placed in the second story—save the difference in the openings and in height.

The dove-tail method of progression (before spoken of) should be adopted; by means of which a man or woman residing in the centre, or ostentatious quarter, may be inferior in fortune to one who occupies a dwelling in the wings, since the best apartments in the wings, renting for six hundred and fifty francs, are more desirable than the poorest in the centre, renting for five hundred. This dove-tailing of values in progressive dwellings provides relief to the extreme series of the wings or winglets, and prevents the distinctions of the simple scale, which would in many instances be offensive to one's self-esteem. Too much care cannot be taken to avoid this evil, which would constitute a germ of discord. —(U. U., iii., 463-469.)

Each agricultural Phalanx forms seven classes in distributing its eatables; they are :

1st.	The heads, . . .	about 50 individuals.	⎫
2nd.	The sick and patriarchs,	„ 50 „	⎪
3rd.	The first class, . .	„ 100 „	⎬ 1500
4th.	The second class, . .	„ 300 „	⎪
5th.	The third class, . .	„ 900 „	⎪
6th.	The children from 2 to 4½,	„ 100 „	⎭
7th.	The caravansary, unlimited number.		
K.	A lot of animals consuming the coarse eatables and the refuse.—(U. U., iii., 48.)		

The consequence is that the dishes of the third class, consisting of the lowest stratum of people, will surpass in delicacy those which at present constitute the delight of our gastronomes. As to the variety of food which will be found upon the tables of the people, it cannot be estimated at less than thirty or forty dishes, renewed by thirds every day, along with a dozen different drinks, varied at each meal.[1]—(Q. M., 246.)

We find in our great cities an imperceptible germ of progressive housekeeping; it is the *Circles or Casinos for men and women;* they are already causing people to desert the insipid family soirée. There one can at a slight cost enjoy balls and concerts, all manner of games, journals, and other kinds of diversion, which would be ten times as costly in a private house. Every pleasure proves economical there both in money and in effort, for the arrangements are left to the official members, as in the progressive household. But the *Circles* or *Casinos* are subject to equality, which impedes the developments of ambition, while the progressive household, being subdivided into rival and unequal groups, opens a vast field to the three ambitious intrigues of *protector, protégé,* and *independent.*—(Q. M., 175.)

One is dazzled by lingering a few moments over a picture of the enormous benefits which would be derived from the union of 300 households, in a single edifice, where they would find apartments at various prices, covered ways from part to part, tables of different classes, varied kinds of occupation—in short, everything that tends to shorten and facilitate labour and to render it attractive.

Let us enter into the details. I shall examine first the advantages of the associative loft and cellar.

The 300 lofts which are to-day used by 300 families of villagers (1500, 1600 individuals) would be replaced by an extensive and salubrious storehouse divided into special compartments for each commodity, and even for every variety of the different species. One could there secure all the advantages of ventilation, dryness, heating, exposure, etc., things which a villager cannot think of

---

[1] The father of a family on reading this sketch will say : "I take pleasure in dining with my wife and my children, and, come what may, I shall maintain this habit which pleases me."   That is a very poor judgment : it pleases him now, in default of anything better, but after he shall have seen the customs of Harmony for two days, and been allured by the intrigues and cabals of the Series, he will wish to dine with his cabalistic committees, and will send his wife and children to the flock, while they on their side will ask for nothing better than to be freed from the dismal family dinner.—(U. U., iii., 447.)

doing ; for it frequently happens that his entire hamlet is poorly conditioned for the preservation of commodities. A Phalanx, on the contrary, selects a favourable locality, both as regards the whole and the details, such as the cellars, lofts, etc.

The outlay for this extensive storehouse in building, walls, timber-work, roofing, doors, pulleys, fire-inspection, guarantees against insects, etc., would amount to scarcely a tenth of that involved in the villagers' 300 lofts, which are limited to one floor, while three could be put under one roof. The associative storehouse would use only ten doors and fastenings, while our villagers use 300 doors ; and likewise of everything else.

It is, above all, in the precautions against fire, epizootics, and damage, that the gain would be immense. Any measure for general security is impracticable among 300 civilised families, some of them too poor, others unskilled or malicious. Accordingly we see, every year, the imprudence of a single household cause the conflagration of a whole village, the contagious infection of all the cattle of the neighbourhood.

The precautions against animals and insects likewise prove illusory in our villages because the entire community does not co-operate ; thus, hunting wolves does not prevent these animals from increasing. If, by dint of care, you destroy the rats in your granaries, you will soon be invaded by those of neighbouring granaries, and of fields which have not been purged by general measures ; these are impossible in civilisation, where even the getting rid of caterpillars cannot be effected, a measure yearly enjoined by the mayors, but never executed. There will not be a handful of caterpillars in the regions cultivated associatively ; that is one of the insects that will disappear after the lapse of three years of combined exploitation.

Combined administration gives rise to a multitude of economies as to doings which we consider productive ; for example, three hundred families of an agricultural village send to the markets, not once, but twenty times in the course of a year. The peasant delights in loitering about in the market-places and taverns ; though he have nothing but a bushel of beans, he spends an entire day in the city. And for the three hundred fam lies, this constitutes an average loss of 6,000 days of labour, not including the cost of transportation, which is twenty times greater than in association, which sells all its commodities in large quantities, since, in that order, purchases are made only for Phalanxes numbering about 1,500 individuals.

While economising in the complication of sales—the abuse of sending three hundred persons to the markets instead of one, conducting three hundred negotiations instead of one,—economy is at the same time effected in the complication of labour. If a canton sells 3,000 quintals of wheat to three other cantons, the work of grinding and baking will not extend to nine hundred householders, but only to three. Thus, after saving 99 per cent. in distributive labour in the sales, this saving will be repeated in the labour and management of the consumer. There will, therefore, be a double saving of 99 per cent. : and how many more of a similar kind will occur !

Let us observe, in this connection, that associative economy is almost always of a composite order ; like that which to the saving of expense to the vendor adds, by way of counter-stroke, the saving of expense to the consumer.

Let us pass from grains to liquids. The three hundred village households have three hundred cellars and vat-chambers, attended to with equal lack of knowledge and of skill. The damage in the cellars is even greater than in the lofts, the handling of liquids being a much more delicate and risky matter than that of solids.

A Phalanx, whether for its wines, its oils, or its dairy products, will have but a single repository.

As for casking, about thirty large casks would suffice, instead of the thousand small ones used by the three hundred civilised families. There would, therefore, be, besides the saving of nine-tenths upon the building, a saving of nineteen-twentieths upon casking, a thing very costly and doubly ruinous to our cultivators : frequently, with a great outlay, they cannot maintain the vessels in their cellars in a salubrious condition, and expose the liquid to

corruption, by a thousand errors which the associative management would avoid.

Wine-making is, of all the branches of agricultural industry,
that in which the civilised are the most deficient. It is impossible
for peasants, and even for good land-owners, to give wine the
proper care.

In the course of the autumn of 1819, the district in which I lived
lost 10,000 puncheons of wine by sprouting, for the weak
qualities of wine require three sorts of attention which it is
impossible to give them in civilisation.

1° Good cellars built in a favourable location, either upon
rocky soil or upon elevated ground exposed to the north. Is the
peasant able to fulfil these conditions? not even the land-owner,
who uses such a cellar as chance has given him.

2° Daily airing of the cellars and casks. We do not see these
precautions observed in a village : the peasant possesses neither
the time, nor the capacity, nor the means. It is only a passional
series of the cellarists who can attend to such duties.

3° Crossing weak wines with those of a strong quality, thus
properly fortifying the former. Neither the peasant nor the
bourgeois can think of providing himself with the warm wines
of Portugal, Spain, Calabria, Cyprus, etc. A Phalanx, which
negotiates for 1,500 persons, corresponds with every country and
readily procures, by the *veracious commercial method,* every
commodity required, and of such quality as it desires.

None of those mishaps which paralyse civilised agriculture will
be found to occur among the Harmonians. Moreover, the reaping
is done in a graduated way ; and when the mingling of what is
green, ripe, and over-ripe is avoided, much less chance is given
to the germs of corruption ; a Phalanx avoids them in every
instance, by appropriating special and enthusiastic groups to each
kind of labour ; by that means they escape the enormous waste
of which our statisticians forget to take account.

There is nothing in which economy is recognised as more
urgently needed than in fuel ; this economy assumes vast proportions in the associative state ; a Phalanx has only five kitchens
in place of three hundred ; namely :

The administrative, or extra ;
The first, second, and third classes.
The provision for animals.

The whole can be supplied by three great fires, which, compared to the 300 fires of a village, brings the economy in fuel to nine-tenths.

It will be no less enormous in shop fires : it will be seen in the treatise upon the passionate Series, that their groups, whether in their relations in domestic or in manufacturing industry, their relations in pleasure, balls, etc., always operate in large companies and in connecting halls or *Seristeries,* furnished with steam-stoves which it is necessary to heat only three hours for the twenty-four. Individual fires are very rare, except in the coldest part of winter, each one as a rule seldom returning to his quarters before the hour of retiring, when he contents himself with a little brasier while undressing.

Moreover, the cold is not felt in the interior of the phalanstery ; every portion of the main buildings is provided with covered galleries, by means of which one can communicate with all parts, sheltered from the inclemencies of the weather. People can go to the workshops, the dining-halls, to balls and assemblies without needing furs or boots, without exposing themselves to colds or inflammations. The closed communication extends even from the phalanstery to the stables, by underground gravelled passages or by galleries supported upon columns at the level of the second floor.

I have just passed in review some of the associative savings : a successive examination of these shows them to amount always to three-fourths or nine-tenths, and frequently to ninety-nine hundredths. We have found it so in the case of the markets, the sale and purchase of commodities ; even in petty concerns which one does not to-day deign to take into account, and which assume great importance when the saving amounts to ninety-nine in a hundred, or even to forty-nine in fifty, like that of the milk-women. If a village is situated near a city, we find that the three hundred families will sometimes send a hundred milk-women with a hundred cans of milk, the sale and transportation of which cause these women to lose a hundred mornings. I have observed that they can be replaced by a small cart drawn by an ass, and driven by a woman; a gain of forty-nine fiftieths. The saving is doubled when we consider that the woman, distributing in two or three great establishments (called progressive households, which will constitute the associative *régime* of the cities), will return home in half the time which it would have taken the hundred women : this is a real gain of ninety-nine per cent., in time and in people.

The instances of saving I have just cited all relate to activities already known and practised; we might enumerate a host of others which turn upon activities to be dispensed with : I shall term them *negative* savings,—in contradistinction to the preceding, which are *positive*, or diminution of labour without abolishment of the service.

Let us define some kind of labour to be dispensed with, or negative gain of Association : there is one that assumes vast proportions, and that is, the precautions against theft.

The danger of theft obliges three hundred families of a village, or at least the hundred in easiest circumstances, to make an un-productive outlay in enclosure—walls, barricades, fastenings, landmarks, dogs, ditches, day and night watchmen, and other means of defence against thieves. These useless and expensive devices will be done away with in Association, which possesses the property of preventing larceny, and dispensing with all precautions against danger. We shall see this farther on.

Under associative conditions, it would be impossible for the thief to reap any profit from the thing stolen, excepting in the case of money ;—but a people who live in ease and are imbued with sentiments of honour do not even conceive any projects for stealing. It will be shown that children, so essentially robbers of fruit, would not, in the associative state, take an apple off a tree.

Let us analyse, in the case of fruit alone, the damage caused by stealing. Everyone has had occasion to observe, in populous cities, the market filled with unripe and very unwholesome fruits, particularly stone-fruits. If the peasants are taken to task for this premature picking, this vegetable murder, every one of them answers : *they will be stolen if I wait for them to get ripe.* We have shown above that such theft vitiates the quality of all wines by the practice of complete and simultaneous gathering, under the public regulation of the time of vintage. Stealing likewise vitiates other fruits, by compelling a premature gathering. On account of reaping not being done at the proper time and in three degrees, in order to avoid the mixing of the green, the ripe, and the over-ripe, it is difficult, indeed impossible, to preserve fruits. This inconvenience conduces, along with the lack of good fruiterers and of scientific methods, to reduce the amount of fruit preserved to one-twentieth, and to a reduction of a like proportion in the cultivation of these vegetable products.—(U. U., iii., 7-17.)

CHAPTER XIII

A THEORY of Groups ! ! !

What is its object? It is to ascertain by what methods the associative bond is established, so impracticable with the customs of civilisation. It can only be organised by the employment of industrial groups and series of groups, holding short sessions; there is no other means.

This is sufficient to indicate how much attention students ought to give to this summary, which is the foundation of the structure. One could not, without reading this chapter, proceed to that of the treatise.

The groups, or elementary modes of social relations, are four in number, in correspondence with the material elements of the universe. Following is the analogical table.

GROUPS.			ELEMENTS.
Major { of Friendship,	unisexual	affection,	Earth
{ of Ambition,	corporative	"	Air
Minor { of Love,	bisexual	"	Aroma
{ of Family,	consanguineous	"	Fire
Pivotal, of Unityism or fusion of bonds			Fire.

The pivotal group is only a composite bond, not an elementary one; it is applicable to each of the other four.

No other bonds can be discovered in the social man. If he does not form any of these four bonds, he becomes, like the wild man of the Aveyron, a brute beast in human shape. He progresses in sociableness (*sociabilité*) only in so far as he succeeds in forming one, or two, or three, or four groups. It is, therefore, by the analysis of groups that the study of the social man should have been initiated,—a thing entirely neglected, in spite of all that is said.

The senses by themselves are not springs of sociableness, for the most influential of them, that of taste, *necessity of nourishment*, urges to anthropophagy. Sociableness, then, depends upon the formation of groups, or passionate leagues.

The four groups exercise influence alternatively in the four phases of life ; each one is dominant in one of the phases, as shown in the following table :

ALTERNATIVE DOMINANCE OF THE GROUPS.

In anterior phase, or childhood,	1 to 15 years, friendship.
In citerior phase, or adolescence,	16 to 35 years, love.
In focal phase, or virility,	36 to 45 years, *love and ambition.*
In ulterior phase, or maturity,	46 to 65 years, ambition.
In posterior phase, or old age,	66 to 80 years, family feeling.

The succession of influences enumerated corresponds to that of bud, flower, fruit, seed,—to the four ages of vegetation.

This table has no need of a commentary. It cannot be disputed that friendship predominates in childhood, as love does in youth ; that ambition prevails in mature life, and that old age, isolated from the world, concentrates itself upon family affection, being incapable of the other three feelings ; for civilised old age is generally too mistrustful to surrender itself to a real friendship : it is justly reproached with abandoning itself completely to egoism, which is the opposite of friendship.[1]—(U. U., iii., 337-339.)

Let us first divide them into such as are harmonious and such as are subversive.

[1] That is an amusing sort of liberalism which desires everything for its own, and nothing for others. Such is the custom in civilised testaments : everything is bequeathed to one's family, as if no other class were worthy of liberality. The priesthood has had the good sense to rise up against this family egoism, and to induce the testators to make less exclusive bequests,— to the parish, to hospitals, to monasteries.

Those who profess to be liberals ought to propagate this tendency in the direction of friendship, and introduce the custom of leaving legacies to classes in their province,—to learned societies and societies of artists, to bodies organised for carrying on public works and improvements. It is unpardonable for a bachelor or a married man whose family is in easy circumstances to make a will exclusively in its favour.—(U. U., iii., 288.)

A harmonious group is a perfectly independent body, united by one or more affections common to the various individuals of which the group is composed.

If a group is harmonious, the *dominant* or real passion is consonant to the *tonic* or apparent passion (*passion d'étalage*).

The group is subversive, when the dominant and the tonic are different.

For instance, nothing is more common than gatherings of pretended friends, each a mass of egoism, with nothing of friendship but its mask, no real motive but interest. Such are fashionable assemblies, where not a shadow of the devotion affected is felt. Each one comes there with designs of personal ambition, gallantry, gluttony, pretending meanwhile to be actuated solely by pure and ardent friendship.

These groups have a *dominant* contradictory to the *tonic*. In fact, their tonic or apparent passion is friendship ; their dominant or real motive is personal interest.

As TONIC, an association of club-men pretend to be absorbed by love of country, fraternity, august philosophy, and the welfare of the sovereign people. As DOMINANT, they are actuated simply by the desire to grow rich, and to gain possession of the public offices.

The contradiction of tonic and dominant constitutes the subversive group, which is the common spring in civilised mechanism. The four groups are ordinarily subversive, and almost never harmonious, or impelled by passions which are at once *dominant* and *tonic.*—(U. U., iii., 341.)

Harmonious or regular groups, those whose dominant is consonant to their tonic, ought to fulfil the following three conditions :

1st. Spontaneous association without compulsory ties, and with no obligations beyond those of decorum.

2nd. Ardent and blind passion for a branch of industry or kind of pleasure common to all the members.

3rd. Boundless devotion to the interests of the group ;

inclination to make sacrifices for the maintenance of the common passion.

This devotion ought to predominate even in the group of the family : alone among the four, it possesses the vice of immutability of material ties. This tie, formed forcibly by blood, will, in Harmony, have to be restored by affection to *spontaneity ;* to be passionate among kindred by blood as it is among associates by choice *(adoptifs).*[1]—(U. U., iii., 341.)

Let us first devote a page•to the elementary ideas of the mainspring of Association, the *series of groups* or *passional series.* It is a union of different groups, each of which works in some SPECIES of a passionate GENUS. Twenty groups, cultivating twenty kinds of roses, form a series of ROSISTS as to genus, and *white-rosists, yellow-rosists, moss-rosists,* as to species.   Such is the sole lever employed in Association.—(U. U., i., 142.)

In every numerous association, the workers must be classed into groups homogeneous in tastes, and these groups affiliated in an ascending and descending Series, in order that the inclinations of each individual may be developed, and their emulation aroused by a methodical opposition of contrasts ;

Emulation, industrial improvement, and, consequently, profits, increase in proportion to the exactitude with which the shades of inclination are graded, and formed into groups which compose a Series.—(U. U., iii., 509.)

[1] Our legislators wish to subordinate the social system to the last of the four groups, that of the Family, which God has almost entirely excluded from influence in social Harmony, because it is a group with a material or forced bond of union, not one of free association, passional, dissoluble at pleasure.

It was befitting people who, in all their calculations, are in contradiction with nature, to take as the pivot of the social mechanism that one of the four groups which ought to have the least influence, since it lacks freedom ; in Harmony, accordingly, it has no active function except when it is absorbed by the other three and acts in their spirit.

Duplicity, being engendered by all constraint, is likely to prevail in proportion to the influence of the family group, which is neither free nor dissoluble ; there is nothing, accordingly, more false than the two societies, the civilised and the patriarchial, in which this group is dominant.   Barbarous society, more sanguinary, more oppressive than ours, is, nevertheless, less false, being less influenced by the Family group, one of the greatest germs of duplicity in the domain of action.   By reason of its indissoluble bond, it is incongruous with the spirit of God, who wishes to govern solely by attraction, or liberty of ties and motives.—(Q. M., 115.)

A passionate series is a union of different groups graded in an ascending and a descending order, passionally joined together by identity of taste for some form of activity, such as the cultivation of a fruit, and appropriating a special group to each variety of labour comprehended in the object to which it is devoted. If it cultivates hyacinths or potatoes, it must form as many groups as there are varieties of hyacinths capable of being cultivated upon its land, and so likewise of the varieties of potatoes.

These dispositions must be regulated by attraction ; each group must be composed only of such members as take part passionally, without having recourse to the mediums of necessity, morality, reason, duty, and compulsion.—(N. M., 52.)

There is nothing less fraternal and less equal than the groups of a passionate series. In order to balance it properly, it must gather together and combine extremes in fortune, in intelligence, in character, etc. ; such as the millionaire and the man without means, fiery and placid natures, the learned man and the ignoramus, old age and youth ; this mixture lacks in nothing more than in equality.

Another condition is that the groups be in irreconcilable rivalry ; that they criticise without mercy the minutest details of each other's work ; that their pretensions be incompatible and in every way distinct, without the slightest fraternity ; that, on the contrary, they organise scissions, jealousies, and intrigues of every description. Such a *régime* will be as far removed from fraternity as it is from equality ; and nevertheless it is this mechanism which will give birth to super-composite liberty, which is in total opposition to philosophic doctrines : [1] they enjoin a contempt for perfidious riches and encouragement of arbitrary traffic or free

[1] We must not persuade ourselves that in Harmony mankind are brothers and friends. It would be robbing life of its salt to cause the shades of opinion, contradictions, antipathies even, to disappear from it. But it must be observed that in the play of the series these disagreements operate only as regards the contact of group with group, and not of individual with individual. It is of little consequence that the groups be irreconcilable, provided there exist bonds of connection between their respective individuals. . . . The more a series is subject to internal discord, the greater the prodigies it performs for external concord.—(*Phalange*, vol. published in 1850, p. 136.)

falsehood. The associative order, or super-composite liberty, requires, on the contrary, love of riches and of boundless luxury, the extirpation of commercial falsehood, and a guarantee of truth in all transactions.

The philosophic or civilised state leads to riches by the practice of falsehood, and to ruin by the practice of truth ; the associative state leads to riches by the practice of truth, and to ruin by resort to falsehood.

Philosophy desires in the domestic and the industrial *régime* the smallest body possible, limited to one man and one woman ; the associative order desires in the domestic *régime* the greatest body possible, comprising about 1,500 persons, who, in place of conjugal indifference, the monotonies of civilisation, and republican fraternity, will be actuated by :

Jealous intrigues and contrasting rivalries, according to the laws of the tenth passion, called *Cabalist* or *dissident ;*

Frequent and habitual change of occupation, according to the laws of the eleventh passion, called *Papillonne* or *alternant ;*

Industrial ardour, general enthusiasm, according to the laws of the twelfth passion, called *Composite* or *coïncident.*—(U. U., ii., 161.)

If the scale of tastes is properly constituted, each group is at odds with those contiguous to it ; consider the series of thirteen groups,

A B C D *e f* G *h i* J L M N.

The group G is very discordant with *f* and *h,* whose tastes it accounts very defective ; it is in semi-discord with the sub-contiguous groups *e, i ;* it only begins to have affinity with D J, C L, B M, which become sympathetic at the third, the fourth, the fifth remove, etc. ; but the neighbouring groups of the scale are antipathetic industrially, jealous, rivals for fame. It is the counterpart of musical relations : a tone does not harmonise with those contiguous to it.

It is by such means alone that those sublime harmonies can be called forth, described under the name of unions (*ralliements*), and whose characteristic is to *absorb egoism and individual dis-*

cords in the accords of the masses ; a characteristic whose special uses in the associative *régime* I have frequently explained.— (U. U., iv., 462.)

In order to attain passional success, or the mechanism of the series, we must bring a great number of series into play, at the least 50 or 60, and at the most 500 ; then shorten their sessions so that every member may figure in a large number of series, attend 50 or 60 of them if possible, Dove-tailing (engrener) them one with the other; that is the condition *sine quâ non.*

In order to fulfil it, numbers must be taken into account. If a certain task requires 50 hours of a gardener's work, detail 50 men to do it; they will only have work for an hour, and each of them will be able, in the course of 50 hours, to engage in 50 occupations instead of one. It is upon this linking or variety of occupations, that is grounded the entire fabric of the passional series and its properties of passional harmony ; is there anything to inspire dread in this doctrine ? It is the doctrine of pleasure. —(U. U., i., 143.)

This, then, is that doctrine of series, pronounced so dreadful by some alarmists. It is limited to observing how three passions derive profit from the harmonies and the discords of a score of groups. Three thousand years have been employed in seeking the art of annihilating discords, and making us all brothers ; could not three hours be devoted to the art of utilising these discords, since it is demonstrated that they cannot be destroyed? God would not have created them, had he not judged them necessary : they are the aliment of the tenth passion.—(U. U., i., 151.)

Every innocent mania is admitted to the rank of laudable and harmonious impulses, provided that its devotees can gather together the nucleus of a series, consisting of at least nine persons, and arranged in a regular group as above.

No matter how comical a fancy may be, it is breveted a useful and respectable passion, if it can offer this feature of corporative union. It has a right to a standard in its reunions, a right to outward insignia for its members, and a place in the ceremonials of a certain degree, province, or region, if it may not figure in those of the Phalanx.   Thus God knows how to attain the goal of unity by the double road—

Of the infinitely small as well as the infinitely great ;

Of the infinitely ridiculous as well as the infinitely charming.—
(U. U., ii., 346-349.)

CHAPTER XIV

In the civilised mechanism we find everywhere composite un-happiness instead of composite charm. Let us judge of it by the case of labour. It is, says the Scripture very justly, a punishment of man : Adam and his issue are condemned to earn their bread by the sweat of their brow. That, already, is an affliction ; but this labour, this ungrateful labour upon which depends the earning of our miserable bread, we cannot even get it ! a labourer lacks the labour upon which his maintenance depends,—he asks in vain for a tribulation ! He suffers a second, that of obtaining work at times whose fruit is his master's and not his, or of being employed in duties to which he is entirely unaccustomed. . . . The civilised labourer suffers a third affliction through the maladies with which he is generally stricken by the excess of labour de-manded by his master. . . . He suffers a fifth affliction, that of being despised and treated as a beggar because he lacks those necessaries which he consents to purchase by the anguish of repugnant labour. He suffers, finally, a sixth affliction, in that he will obtain neither advancement nor sufficient wages, and that to the vexation of present suffering is added the perspective of future suffering, and of being sent to the gallows should he demand that labour which he may lack to-morrow.—(Man., 208.)

Labour, nevertheless, forms the delight of various creatures, such as beavers, bees, wasps, ants, which are entirely at liberty to prefer inertia : but God has provided them with a social mechanism which attracts to industry, and causes happiness to be found in industry. Why should he not have accorded us the same favour as these animals ? What a difference between their industrial condition and ours! A Russian, an Algerian, work from fear of the lash or the bastinado; an Englishman, a Frenchman, from fear of the famine which stalks close to his poor household; the Greeks and the Romans, whose freedom has been vaunted to us, worked as slaves, and from fear of punishment, like the negroes in the colonies to-day.—(U. U., ii., 249.)

Associative labour, in order to exert a strong attraction upon people, will have to differ in every particular from the repulsive conditions which render it so odious in the existing state of things. It is necessary, in order that it become attractive, that associative labour fulfil the following seven conditions :

1° That every labourer be a partner, remunerated by dividends and not by wages.

2° That every one, man, woman, or child, be remunerated in proportion to the three faculties, *capital, labour,* and *talent.*

3° That the industrial sessions be varied about eight times a day, it being impossible to sustain enthusiasm longer than an hour and a half or two hours in the exercise of agricultural or manufacturing labour.

4° That they be carried on by bands of friends, united spontaneously, interested and stimulated by very active rivalries.

5° That the workshops and husbandry offer the labourer the allurements of elegance and cleanliness.

6° That the division of labour be carried to the last degree, so that each sex and age may devote itself to duties that are suited to it.

7° That in this distribution, each one, man, woman, or child, be in full enjoyment of the right to labour or the right to engage in such branch of labour as they may please to select, provided they give proof of integrity and ability.

⋈ [1] Finally, that, in this new order, people possess a guarantee of well-being, of a minimum sufficient for the present and the future, and that this guarantee free them from all uneasiness concerning themselves and their families.

---

[1] The sign ⋈, in the language of Fourier, serves to designate that which is "pivotal," that is to say, fundamental, in enumeration.

We find all these properties combined in the associative mechanism, whose discovery I make public.—(U. U., ii., 15.)

We know what effect association and ownership have upon one engaged in industrial occupations. He appears sluggish while working for wages, for others' benefit ; but the moment commercial association has inoculated him with the spirit of ownership and participation, he becomes a prodigy of diligence, and they say of him : "*He is not the same man ; one cannot recognise him.*" Why ? Because he has become a COMPOSITE owner. His emulation is so much the more valuable in that he works for a whole body of associates and not himself alone, as is the case with the small cultivator, so highly lauded by morality, and who is in reality nothing but an egoist :—poor morality, which in all things has an unlucky hand, can praise only the sources of vice. It was natural enough that it should end by praising free trade or the rule of falsehood.

The emulative influence of association, noticeable even under existing conditions, will be powerful in a very different way in Harmony, where it will be sustained by all the noblest sentiments, as will be seen further on. But in order to humour the pre-dominant spirit of the civilised, simplism (*simplisme*), or the passion for simple motives, I shall, in this prelude, consider the emulation of the poor only in its relation to pecuniary interest, without speaking of noble motives, such as friendship, glory, patriotism, etc., which enter into every part of the industrial mechanism of the passional series.

He ought to love work, say our sages : yes ! but how go about it ? What is lovable about it in civilisation for nine-tenths of mankind, who reap only weariness from it and no benefits ? Consequently, it is generally shunned by the rich, who engage only in the lucrative and agreeable side of it, in direction. How cause it to be liked by the poor, when it cannot be rendered pleasant to the rich ?—(U. U., iii., 519.)

In order to attain happiness, it is necessary to introduce it into the labours which engage the greater part of our lives. Life is a long torment to one who pursues occupations without attraction.

Morality teaches us to love work : let it know, then, how to render work lovable, and, first of all, let it introduce luxury into husbandry and the workshop.   If the arrangements are poor, repulsive, how arouse industrial attraction ?

In work, as in pleasure, variety is evidently the desire of nature. Any enjoyment prolonged, without interruption, beyond two hours, conduces to satiety, to abuse, blunts our faculties, and exhausts pleasure.   A repast of four hours will not pass off without excess ; an opera of four hours will end by cloying the spectator.   Periodical variety is a necessity of the body and of the soul, a necessity in all nature ;   even the soil requires alteration of seeds, and seed alteration of soil.   The stomach will soon reject the best dish if it be offered every day, and the soul will be blunted in the exercise of any virtue if it be not relieved by some other virtue.

If there is need of variety in pleasure after indulging in it for two hours, so much the more does labour require this diversity, which is continual in the associative state, and is guaranteed to the poor as well as the rich.—(U. U., i., 147.)

The chief source of light-heartedness among Harmonians is the frequent change of sessions.   Life is a perpetual torment to our workmen, who are obliged to spend twelve, and frequently fifteen, consecutive hours in some tedious labour.   Even ministers are not exempt ; we find some of them complain of having passed an entire day in the stupefying task of affixing signatures to thousands of official vouchers.   Such wearisome duties are unknown in the associative order ; the Harmonians, who devote an hour, an hour and a half, or at most two hours, to the different sessions, and who, in these short sessions, are sustained by cabalistic impulses and by friendly union with selected associates, cannot fail to bring and to find cheerfulness everywhere.

Let us delineate this variation by a table exhibiting a day of two Harmonians, one poor and one rich.

Lugas' Day in the Month of June.

Hours.

At 3½   rising,   getting ready.

At 4   attendance at a stable group.

At 5   ——— at a gardeners' group.

At 7   *breakfast.*

At 7½   ——— at the reapers' group.

At 9½   ——— at the vegetable-growers' group under cover.

At 11   ——— at the stable series.

At 1   Dinner.

At 2   ——— at the rural series.

At 4   ——— at a manufacturing group.

At 6   ——— at the watering series.

At 8   ——— at 'Change.

At 8½   *Supper.*

At 9   ——— at resorts of amusement.

At 10   *bed-time.*

I shall delineate, framed in between five meals, the day of a rich man, practising more varied occupations than the one above, who is one of the villagers enrolled in the beginning.

Mondor's Day in Summer.

Hours.   Sleep from 10½ in the evening to 3 o'clock in the morning.

At 3½   rising, getting ready.

At 4   court of public levee, news of the night.

At 4½   the *délite*, first meal, followed by the industrial parade.

At 5½   attendance at the hunting group.

At 7   ——— at the fishing group.

Hours.		
At 8	*breakfast,*	newspapers.
At 9		attendance at an agricultural group under cover.
At 10	——	at mass.
At 10½	——	at the pheasantry group.
At 11½	———	at the library.
At 1	DINNER.	
At 2½	———	at the group of cold green-houses.
At 4	———	at the group of exotic plants.
At 5	——	at the group of fish-ponds.
At 6	*luncheon*	in the fields.
At 6½	————	at the group of merinoes.
At 8	——	at 'Change.
At 9	SUPPER,	fifth repast.
At 9½	———	court of the arts, ball, theatre, receptions.
At 10½	*bed-time.*	

We find in the table but a brief place allowed for sleep : the Harmonians will sleep very little ; perfected hygiene, coupled with variety of employments, will accustom them not to get fatigued in their labours ; their bodies will not be exhausted in the course of the day, will need but a small amount of sleep, and will accustom themselves to it from childhood by an abundance of pleasures for which the day cannot be sufficiently long.

In such an order, attraction, by reason of its intensity, requires some easing, some calm sessions, such as that of the library, eighth in the above table. The civilised order institutes recreations as a relaxation from annoying labour; the associative order provides only for a slackening of pleasure.[1]—(N. M., 67, 68.)

[1] Upon beholding this associative fairyland, these harmonies, these prodigies, this sea of delights, created simply by attraction or divine impulse, we shall see aroused a frenzy of enthusiasm for God, author of so beautiful an order ; and perfectible, infamous civilisation, will be loaded with universal malediction. Its political and moral libraries will be spat upon, torn up in the first moment of anger, and delivered over to the meanest uses, until they are reprinted with a critical commentary, facing the text, to make it the enduring laughing-stock of the human race.—(N. M., 287.)

The radical evil of our industrial system is the employment of the labourer in a single occupation, which runs the risk of coming to a stand-still. The fifty thousand workmen of Lyons who are beggars to-day (besides fifty thousand women and children), would be scattered over two or three hundred phalanxes, which would make silk their principal article of manufacture, and which would not be thrown out by a year or two of stagnation in that branch of industry. If at the end of that time their factory should fail completely, they would start one of a different kind, without having stopped work, without ever making their daily subsistence dependent upon a continuation or suspension of outside orders. —(F. I. [d. s.].)

In a progressive series all the groups acquire so much the more skill in that their work is greatly subdivided, and that every member engages only in the kind in which he professes to excel. The heads of the Series, spurred on to study by rivalry, bring to their work the knowledge of a student of the first rank. The subordinates are inspired with an ardour which laughs at all obstacles, and with a fanaticism for the maintenance of the honour of the Series against rival districts. In the heat of action they accomplish what seems humanly impossible, like the French grenadiers who scaled the rocks of Mahon, and who, upon the day following, were unable, in cold blood, to clamber up the rock which they had assailed under the fire of the enemy. Such are the progressive Series in their work ; every obstacle vanishes before the intense pride which dominates them ; they would grow angry at the word *impossible*, and the most daunting kinds of labour, such as managing the soil, are to them the lightest of sports. If we could to-day behold an organised district, behold at early dawn thirty industrial groups issue in state from the palace of the Phalanx, and spread themselves over the fields and the workshops, waving their banners with cries of triumph and impatience, we should think we were gazing at bands of madmen intent upon putting the neighbouring districts to fire and sword. Such will be the athletes who will take the place of our mercenary and languid workmen, and who will succeed in making ambrosia and nectar grow upon a soil which yields only briers and tares to the feeble hands of the civilised.—(Q. M., 244.)

CHAPTER XV

LITTLE HORDES (LES PETITES HORDES)

FRESH souls, especially those of the young, possess an energy in the exercise of patriotic virtues which is not found in people of the world, who are ready to waver and tack about to obtain a sinecure.

In view of this, it is at once evident that the fathers are inferior to the children in the exercise of the virtues called patriotic.

Association knows how to profit by this inclination of youth to devotion to society ; it knows how to employ childhood in positions where the fathers would be remiss ; among others, in positions involving repugnant labour.

This repugnance is to-day overcome by the inducement of money ; but it will be overcome by attraction, in an order of things in which pleasure will be the prime mover in the social mechanism.

The *régime* of attraction would fail utterly, unless it succeeded in attaching powerful baits to repellent kinds of labour, which can only be carried on in civilisation by the inducement of wages.—(U. U., iv., 138.)

Some mercantile champion will object, that if Harmony is so immensely rich, as shown by the tables given of the thirty-fold relative increase, it could appropriate a large amount to the remuneration of repugnant labour. Such will be the case in emasculated (partial) association, which cannot develop the great springs of attraction ; but in complete Harmony not a farthing will be appropriated to the payment of unclean labour : it would be subversive of the entire mechanism of high attraction, which should conquer the very strongest feelings of repugnance by *esprit de corps.*—(U. U., iii., 531.)

Why is childhood selected for the chief *rôle* in the mechanism of general amity? It is because children, among the affective passions, are devoted to honour and friendship. Neither love nor the family-feeling divert them from those sentiments : it is among them, therefore, that we ought to find friendship in all its purity, and to give it the noblest spur, that of social unitary charity, preventing, thereby, the debasement of the lower classes, through the encroachment of abject duties, and maintaining amity between the rich and the poor.

In the different chapters treating of the Series, I have demonstrated that if there were a single kind of labour which was despised, considered ignoble and degrading for the class that engaged in it, the inferior duties would soon sink into disrepute in every branch of industry, in the stables, the kitchen, rooms, workshops, etc. : the debasement would spread from one sort of labour to another ; the contempt for labour would be gradually revived, and the result be that, as in civilisation, those people would be termed *comme il faut* who do nothing, are good for nothing. Then the time would come when this wealthy class would no longer take any part in the industrial Series, and would disdain to entertain any social relations with the classes of the poor.

It is the part of childhood to preserve the social body from this evil, undertaking as a body all duties held in disdain, by labouring for a mass and not for an individual (except attending the sick, which can only be entrusted to a body of mature persons, that of the infirmaries ; however, the Little Hordes will take part by doing the dirty work).

It is to that age only we can turn to have the repugnant part of labour performed, by means of indirect attraction.

The love of dirt which prevails in children is only an uncultivated germ, like wild fruit ; it must be refined by applying to it two forces—that of the *unitary religious spirit* and that of *corporative honour*. Supported by these two impulses, repugnant occupations will become games, having INDIRECT COMPOSITE attraction. This condition, set forth in the preceding chapter, is found to be satisfied by the two allurements I have just indicated. For a long time I committed the error of censuring this comical peculiarity of children, and of endeavouring to have it disappear in the mechanism of the passionate Series ; that was acting like a Titan, who wishes to change the work of God. I achieved no success until I adopted the attitude of planning in agreement with attraction ; seeking to utilise the inclinations of childhood, such as Nature has created them. This calculation gave me the corporation which I have just described ; it practises. corporatively the only branch of charity remaining in Harmony ; there are no longer any poor to be succoured, any captives to be ransomed and delivered from prison ; there is nothing, therefore, left for children but to take up the domain of unclean labour,— charity of high statesmanship, since it preserves from contempt the lowest industrial classes, and in the end the intermediate classes. It establishes, thus, the *fraternity* dreamed of by the philosophers, the spontaneous drawing together of all classes.

If, in such an order, the masses are refined, upright, above want, the great can no longer entertain a feeling of mistrust or of contempt for them. A friendly enthusiasm, therefore, is aroused in all the industrial groups, where the masses necessarily mingle with the great. Thus the dream is realised, which wishes to make all mankind a family of brothers.

This precious union would cease the moment one class of labour were held in disdain, disparaged : for instance, if there were paid boot-blacks in Harmony, those children, and consequently their parents, would be counted an inferior class, not admissible in a committee of the Series, in which the rich are members.

If that kind of service is accounted ignoble, the Little Hordes take charge of it and ennoble it. For the rest, it is rarely necessary to clean one's shoes in Harmony, thanks to the covered ways.

They are always up and about at 3 o'clock in the morning,

cleaning the stables, attending to the animals, working in the slaughter-houses, where they are on the watch to see that no unnecessary suffering be ever inflicted upon the animals put to death.[1]—(U. U., iv., 159, 163.)

The Little Hordes have, as one of their duties, the incidental repairing of the highways, that is, the daily maintenance of the surface-roads. The highways, in Harmony, are regarded as salons of unity; and, consequently, the Little Hordes, by virtue of their unitary charity, watch over the cleanliness and the ornamentation of the roadways.

It is to the *amour propre* of the Little Hordes that Harmony will be beholden for having, the world over, highways more sumptuous than the walks of our flower-gardens. They will be lined with trees and shrubs, even flowers, and watered up to the side-walk.

If a post-route sustain the slightest damage, the alarm is sounded instantly, and a tocsin of the tower of order apprises the Argot, who proceeds, by the light of torches if necessary, to make pro-visional repairs, and to hoist an accident-signal over the place, for fear that the damage may not be noticed by some travellers, and give rise to an accusation against the canton of having bad " *sacripants*." It would likewise be accused of having bad " *chenapans*,"[2] if a vicious reptile, serpent or viper, were dis-covered, or a croaking of frogs heard, in proximity to the high-roads.

In spite of their labour being the most difficult, through lack of *direct* attraction, the Little Hordes receive the lowest remuneration of all the Series. They would not accept anything if it were " be-coming" in association to accept no share; they take only the smallest; that does not, however, prevent any of their members from obtain-ing the largest shares in other occupations : but in virtue of their

---

[1] See chapter, *Des Animaux*.

[2] In the vocabulary of Fourier, each one of the Little Hordes has a *nom de guerre*, according with the species of labour to which it devotes itself, and among these names there figure those of " *sacripants* " and "*chenapans*."— Ch. G.

being philanthropic unitary bodies, they have as their law the *indirect* contempt of riches, and devotion to repugnant labour, which they perform as a point of honour.—(U. U., iv., 149, 150.)

I have already remarked that indications of charitable devotion to abject duties are found even among monarchs, and that on Holy Thursday sovereigns are seen washing the feet of a dozen poor people,—a duty by which the monarch thinks himself honoured, on account of the abjectness of the service. Now, when there shall be a corporation of high degree, devoted to the exercise of all the abject duties, none of these will in reality be such ; without this condition, no binding together of the rich class and the poor.

If it is demonstrated that the religious spirit engenders a devotion to general charity, such as is found among the Redemptorist Fathers and other societies, all that need be done is to make use of this inclination, in accordance with the exigencies of the new order ; and even should the corporation of the Little Hordes not appear to be the most efficacious arrangement, it would be none the less certain *that the principle of industrial charity, only alloyed with the religious spirit,* exists among us; and if I have erred in the application, the use, the customs and laws of the body of unitary charity, the critics ought to exert themselves to make better use of an impulse whose existence they cannot dispute; to invent a sect better able to do away with the obstacle of industrial disgust for unclean labour.

However, the Harmonians, more judicious than we in the theory and the practice of charity, will not apply that virtue to useless ceremonies, such as washing the feet of the poor, which they could very well do themselves, or employing a confessor with an income of 50,000 francs to detach a criminal from the gallows. When there shall no longer exist either beggars or people to be hanged, they can no longer serve for calculations of ostentatious charity. All those practices, laudable as to intention and as examples, are only the abortions of a charitable policy. It ought to be applied to effect the drawing together of the classes at the extremes, whom nothing càn conciliate in civilisation, because that order is a failure.[1]—(U. U., iv., 393, 394.)

[1] For the exercise of this " industrial charity," Fourier had recourse also to the creation of a body of vestals, a kind of sisters of charity. The following are his principal passages upon the subject.

The Romans, aside from their cruelty towards seduced vestals, had a happy idea in making these priestesses an object of popular idolatry, a class intermediate between man and divinity. The Harmonians likewise confide to them the keeping of the *sacred fire*, not of a material fire, object of a vain superstition, but of a fire really sacred, that of the manners, loyal and generous, of industrial Attraction.—(N. M., 228.)

If the vestals occupy the first rank, it is because in young girls of sixteen to eighteen years nothing commands higher esteem then a virginity beyond doubt, a genuine, unvarnished decorum, an ardent devotion to useful and charitable duties, an active emulation in worthy studies and in the fine arts. All these qualities combined, in a society of about thirty young girls in every phalanx, must gain unreserved public favour. Accordingly, the vestals, in Harmony, are an object of general idolatry, even for children, for they are the allies of the Little Hordes, and co-operators in their charitable labours, excepting in those of an unclean nature.

They take part as a body, and in conjunction with the Little Hordes, in all the urgent duties for which the Administration, in cases of danger like that of an impending storm, causes an alarm to be sounded for those who can quit their labours. Everywhere where the public interest is in danger, the body of Vestals and the Argot are the first on the spot.

They receive, by way of associative remuneration, only half of the mediocre dividend allotted to the Argot, whose duties are both more numerous and more arduous, and with whom they are associates in charity in the services required in the morning.

Possessing so many titles to the favour of youth and mature age, it is not astonishing that they should be the object of a semi-religious worship.

The Harmonians will not be guilty of the inconsistency of creating vestals of one sex and not of the other ; that would be imitating the contradiction in our customs, which prescribes chastity to the girls and fornication to the boys. This is to provoke on the one hand what is prohibited on the other,—a duplicity worthy of civilisation.—(U. U., iv., 235, 236.)

CHAPTER XVI

DOMESTIC SERVICE

NOTHING is more opposed to concord than the existing condition of the class of domestics and that of wage-earners. By reducing these masses of the poor to a state bordering upon slavery, civilisation imposes, by reflex action, chains upon those who appear to rule the others. Thus, the great do not dare to amuse themselves openly during the years when the people are suffering from want. The rich are subject to individual as well as to collective servitude. Many a man of wealth with us is frequently a slave to his valets ; while the valet himself in Harmony enjoys perfect independence, although the rich are served with a zeal and a devotion, of which not even a shadow can be found in civilisation : let us explain this Harmony.

No member in composite Harmony engages in individual service ; and, nevertheless, the poorest man has fifty pages constantly at his command. This state of things, a statement of which causes at first an outcry against its impossibility, as is the case with every feature of the Serial mechanism, may be readily understood.

In a Phalanx, domestic service, like every other function, is carried on by Series, which appropriate a group to each variety of labour. These Series, while engaged in service, bear the title of *pages* (*pages et pagesses*). We give this title to those who serve kings ; it ought, with much better reason, to be applied to those who serve a Phalanx ; for, indeed, it is serving God to serve the Phalanx *collectively ;* and it is thus that domestic service is regarded in Harmony. If, as to-day, this primordial branch of industry were disparaged, passional equilibrium would become an impossibility.

To this ideal ennoblement of service is added a real ennoblement, by the suppression of individual dependence, which would debase a man by subjecting him to another's caprices.

The industrial cabals of the gardens, the orchards, the opera, workshops, etc., procuring a host of friends to each person, he is sure of finding in every group of pages some who would serve him with affection. The poor enjoy this advantage as well as the rich ; and the man without means finds a host of affectionate attendants as ready to minister to him as to a prince, because *it is never the individual served that pays those who serve him.* A page would be ignominiously discharged if it were known that he had secretly received a gratuity from those he had served. It is the Phalanx which compensates the body of pages, with a dividend taken from the two shares of labour and talent ; a dividend which this Series distributes among its different members in amounts proportioned to their proved ability and assiduity.

Personal independence is therefore fully assured, since each page is assigned to the service of the Phalanx, and not to that of the individual, who is, for that reason, served with affection,—a pleasure which even the rich cannot procure in civilisation, for if you pay a valet generously in order to secure his attachment, ambition will render him indifferent, ungrateful, and often treacherous. This danger is unknown in Harmony, where each one is assured of the friendship of the different pages, who select his service by preference, with the liberty of leaving it in case of a cooling off, and without entering into any pecuniary arrangements with him.

There is, therefore, nothing either mercenary or servile in domestic service in Harmony, and a group of chambermaids is like all the other groups, a free and honourable society which receives a share of the gross product of the Phalanx, proportioned to the importance of its work.—(U. U., iii., 526-530.)

CHAPTER XVII

In conformity with the thesis of counter-swing of movement, association should have the property of assembling productive armies, as civilisation assembles destructive ones.

And, in opposition to the civilised order, which enlists its heroes by putting chains around their necks, the associative order will enlist theirs by the allurement of *fêtes* and pleasures which are unknown in the existing state of things, where an army of a hundred thousand men knows no other collective pleasure but that of destroying, burning, pillaging, and ravishing.

In spite of the jeremiads upon the penurious condition of the finances, every state commands immense masses of capital when it wishes to gather and provision these destructive bodies. I have heard a Russian engineer say, that at the siege of Rustchuk, in 1811, every bomb thrown into that city cost Russia 400 francs, on account of the expense of transportation. What an outlay for the destruction of men and buildings! What a fortunate change would it be to an order of things which would assemble such bodies for useful undertakings!

How is it that our constructors of utopias have not dared to dream of this one : *an assemblage of 500,000 men employed in construction instead of destruction !* After all, the expenditure would be much smaller for a productive army ; and, besides the saving in slaughtered men, burnt cities, devastated fields, we should have the saving of the cost of equipment, and the benefit of the work accomplished.

It is for the lack of industrial armies that civilisation is unable to produce anything great, and fails in all undertakings of any extent ; formerly it accomplished great things by employing hosts of slaves who worked by dint of the lash and of torture. But if works like the Pyramids and Lake Moeris must be drenched with the tears of 500,000 unfortunates, they are monuments of opprobrium, and not trophies of civilisation.

The greatness of Harmony consists as much in the vastness of its undertakings as in the rapidity of their accomplishment, which could not be obtained from a body of slaves and wage-earners, all agreed in shirking labour. The Harmonians, for whom it is transformed into a *fête*, a matter of pride, bring so much the greater activity to bear upon it, in that the number of athletes facilitates its progress.—(U. U., iii., 559, 562.)

They will execute works the mere thought of which would freeze our mercenary souls with horror. For instance, the combined order will undertake the conquest of the great desert of Sahara ; they will attack it at various points by ten and twenty millions of hands if necessary, and by dint of transporting earth, cultivating the soil and planting trees every here and there, they will succeed in rendering the land moist, the sand firm, and in replacing the desert by fruitful regions. They will construct canals navigable by vessels, where we cannot make even ditches for irrigation, and great ships will sail not only across isthmuses like those of Suez and Panama,[1] but even in the interior of continents, as from the Caspian Sea to the Sea of Azov, of Aral, the Persian Gulf ; they will navigate from Quebec to the five great lakes ; finally, from the sea to all the great lakes whose length equals a quarter of their distance to the sea.—(Q. M., 263.)

[1] All narrow and obstructive isthmuses, like those of Panama, Parry, Malacca, will be crossed in the eighth period by canals accommodating vessels adapted to long ocean voyages, of 600 tons burden, and carrying 24 cannon ; that is, canals having 20 feet of water.—(U. U., ii., 97.)

CHAPTER XVIII

DISTRIBUTION

WE are approaching the most important problem of Harmony, that of distribution, balanced and graduated in accordance with the industrial faculties of LABOUR, CAPITAL, and TALENT. The social bond would be broken the very first year, if there were a miscarriage in this particular, and if every one of the members, man, woman, or child, were not convinced that they had received a just share of the three kinds of dividends allotted to those functions.

The civilised order is incapable of making a just distribution except in the case of capital, which is remunerated in proportion to its investment ; that is a problem in arithmetic, and requires no genius ; the Gordian knot of the social mechanism is the rewarding each one for labour and talent. That is the stumbling-block which has dismayed all the ages and blocked investigation.

To evade this double problem of distribution, the Owen sect brings into play the community of goods, the giving over to the whole body of all profit outside of the revenue of the shares. This is to acknowledge that it dares not confront the problem of association.—(N. M., 166.)

It is through their impulses of cupidity that all the Harmonians will be led to this even-handed justice.

Such is the triumph of that cupidity so maligned by the moralists ; God would not have given us that passion, had he not foreseen its use in the general equilibrium. I have already demonstrated that gluttony, equally proscribed by the philosophers, becomes the path of wisdom and industrial concord in the passionate Series. It will be seen that cupidity produces the same effect there, that it leads to distributive justice, and that, in creating our passions, *God did well all that he did.*—(N. M., 309.)

If every Harmonian devoted himself, like the civilised, to a single calling; if he were only a mason, only a carpenter, only a gardener, each one would come to the distributive sessions with the scheme of making his calling prevail, of having the principal share adjudged to the masons if he is a mason, to the carpenters if he is a carpenter, etc.; such would be the course of all the civilised; but in Harmony, where every one, man or woman, is a member of about forty Series, nobody is interested in making one of them prevail over the others; each one, even in his own interest, is obliged to calculate in a manner the reverse of that of the civilised, and to vote in all directions for equity. Let us demonstrate the fact under the aspect of interest and under that of vainglory.

Alcippus is a member of 36 Series, which he divides into three orders, A, B, C. In the 12 of the order A, he is an old member, and is in the first rank, both as regards importance and claims to emolument; in the 12 of the order C, he is a new member, entitled to expect but a slender share; and in the 12 of the order B, he occupies an intermediate position as to time and expectations. These are the three classes of opposite interests, stimulating Alcippus in three different directions, and compelling him, *through interest and through self-love,* to decide in favour of rigorous justice.—(U. U., iv., 529.)

1° *The greater the number of Series frequented,* the greater is the interest of the individual belonging to so many Series, not to sacrifice them all to a single one, and to uphold the interests of 40 companies that he cherishes, against the pretensions of each one of them.

2° *The shorter and rarer the sessions,* the greater facility does the individual possess of enrolling himself in a large number of Series, whose influence would cease to be balanced, if any of them, by long and frequent meetings, should absorb the time and solicitude of the members, and arouse an exclusive affection.

This mechanism, as regards distribution, possesses the inestimable properties :

Of absorbing individual cupidity in the collective interests of a Series, and of absorbing the collective pretensions of each Series in the individual interests which each member has in a host of other Series.[1]—(U. U., iv., 533, 534.)

Each Series, being a PARTNER and not a TENANT of the Phalanx, receives a share not of the proceeds of its own labour, but of that of all the Series, and its compensation is proportioned to the rank it occupies in the table divided into three classes, *necessity, utility, pleasure.*

For instance, a certain Series which cultivates cereals does not receive either a half, a third, or a fourth of the proceeds of the grain that has been reaped : this grain enters into the mass of the entire product sold or consumed, and if the Series which has produced it is recognised as being of great importance in industry, it is compensated by a share of the first order in its class.

---

[1] *Harmonic Medicine.* In civilisation a physician's earnings are proportioned to the number of sick he treats ; it suits him, therefore, to have much sickness prevail and that the ailments should be protracted, particularly among the wealthy class.

The opposite is the case in Harmony ; physicians are compensated by a dividend of the general product of the Phalanx. The rate of this dividend is conditional: it increases by one, two, three, four, six ten-thousandths, or decreases in like proportions, according to the *collective* and *comparative* state of health of the whole Phalanx. The fewer the cases of sickness and death in the course of a year, the larger will be the dividend allotted to the physicians. Their services are estimated by the results, and by comparison with the sanitary statistics of phalanxes having the same climatic conditions.

The interest of Harmonian doctors is the same as that of life-insurance men ; they are interested in preventing and not in treating disease ; accordingly they keep active watch that nothing should endanger the health of any class, that the Phalanx should contain fine-looking specimens of old age, and hearty, robust children, and that mortality should be reduced to a minimum.

Dentists calculate in a like manner in regard to teeth,—the less they have to do with them, the greater their emolument ; accordingly, they take assiduous care of the teeth of child and parent.

In brief, it is to the interest of men in these professions that everyone be provided with a good appetite, a good stomach, a good set of teeth ; if, as with us, they were in the position of having to calculate upon individual illness, their work would be characterised by duplicity of action, opposition of individual to collective interest, as in the civilised mechanism, which is a universal warfare of individuals against the mass. And our political sciences have the hardihood to talk of unity of action !—(N. M., 171, 172.)

The Series that produces cereals evidently belongs to the first class, or that of necessity. But in the class of necessity, about five different orders may be distinguished, and it is probable that the raising of grain will, at the highest, belong to the third order : I do not say the first, because the labour involved in the cultivation and handling of grain is in nowise repugnant, and ought to be ranked after the kinds of labour that are so, and which belong to the first of the five orders of necessity. The work of the Little Hordes stands first of all. Then follows that of butchering, so far as it deals with the disgusting part of the business.

The office of butcher is held in high esteem in Harmony : great affection is entertained for animals, and there is a feeling of obligation to those who have the courage to kill them while taking all imaginable precautions to save them from suffering, and even from becoming cognisant of the idea of death.[1]

Other callings little respected among us, like that of sick-nurses, enjoy the highest consideration in Harmony. The same is the case with wet-nurses : their work being repellent, ought to be ranked above that of tillage, and to constitute, along with the labour of the Little Hordes, the section of the first order in the class of necessity.

In a word, the classing of the Series is determined according to general fitness, and not according to the product. Let us state the principle more exactly : their priority of rank is estimated by a ratio compounded of the following bases :

1. In direct ratio of the contributions to the bonds of unity, to the workings of the social mechanism.

2. In mixed ratio of the repugnant obstacles.

3. In inverse ratio of the amount of attraction which an industry is capable of yielding.

1° *Direct title ;* CONTRIBUTION TO UNITY. The object is to maintain the association which is the source of so much wealth and happiness ; that Series, therefore, is of the highest value, which, PRODUCTIVE or UNPRODUCTIVE, most effectively aids in

---

[1] See chapter, *Des Animaux.*

fastening the social bond. Such is the Series of the Little Hordes, without which the mechanism of the higher Harmony would be destroyed, and the union through friendship be impossible. It is first, therefore, by direct title, or contribution to unity, as well as by the two other basic titles.

2° *Inverse title ;* AMOUNT OF ATTRACTION. The greater the attraction aroused by any species of labour, the smaller is its *pecuniary* value : according to this, it would seem that the opera and orchards should be two series belonging to the third class, or the class of pleasure. The Series of orchards is relegated to that rank because it has only an inverse title, contributing no more to unity than any other branch of agricultural labour. But the Series of the opera contributes specially to unity by its property of fitting the child for all material harmonies : this Series, therefore, has a double title to be regarded valuable, direct and inverse, and takes position in the first ranks of the category of necessity.

3° *Mixed title ;* REPUGNANT OBSTACLES, such as the work of miners, or attendants upon the sick and wet-nurses. An obstacle purely industrial is often a source of amusement ; it is a matter of sport for athletes ; but one cannot make a sport of repugnance which fatigues the senses, such as the cleaning of a sewer, descending into a mine : you can overcome it by a point of honour, as is done by the Little Hordes and sick-nurses ; it is none the less an offence to the senses ; while simple fatigue without disgust, like that of a man who climbs pear-trees and cherry-trees, may become mere child's-play and a real pleasure. Hence it is that the associative order regards only repugnant fatigue as meritorious.

It is by properly combining the above three rules that we succeed in classifying justly and exactly the ranks of each Series, as regards their claims upon the pecuniary dividend, whose distribution is not a purely arithmetical task.—(U. U., iv., 519, 525.)

Besides, a slight inaccuracy in valuation would not be prejudicial to anyone ; for we know that if a person receives more in one Series, less in another, he comes out about even, and in that case there is no real injury.

Let us add that if an injury were *involuntarily* inflicted upon a

Series, a result which might occur without intention, and as a consequence of some general error, it would very soon be detected by the diminution of attraction ; desertion and indifference would ensue : whence it would be decided to augment the attraction of the Series, either by modifying its assortment of characters, or passional key-board, or by granting it a provisional indemnity from the reserve-fund, or by raising it in " degree " at the distribution of the ensuing year. Thus the involuntary errors which might be committed would be rectified as soon as they were perceived. Lack of experience and defects in attraction would occasion a good many such errors in the beginning ; but in less than three years, there will have been obtained experimental and positive data of all the minute details of equilibrium, and the work of distribution will be merely a familiar routine after the third year. —(U. U., iv., 532.)

To these numerous advantages there is added one that is even more unknown in the existing state, and which our famous friends of commerce and circulation could never have been able to compass ; it is the faculty of converting all immovable effects into movable, circulating ones, realisable at will.

Every Phalanx buys up shares, on demand, at the rate of the last appraisement, adding interest for the portion of the year which has elapsed : thus a man, though he possessed a hundred millions, can in an instant realise his entire fortune, without the loss of a farthing, or fees for exchange, or charges for sale. He receives, besides, a part of the interest or current dividend of the year, just as he would receive it upon a negotiable bond on which the interest is reckoned by the day.

Shares constitute a value much more real than do to-day landed property and specie ; for specie in civilisation may be stolen, and does not in itself yield anything unless it is invested. A land share, in Harmony, yields a great deal without investment or risk ; it cannot be lost either through theft, or misplacement, or fire ; its ownership being certified in three registers deposited in two main-buildings of the Phalanx, and in one belonging to some Congress of the vicinity. Transfers not being valid unless with the consent of the registered owner, he runs no risk through theft, mislaying, fire, even through earthquake ; for an earthquake could never swallow the registers bestowed in different places, nor the copy which is deposited in the provincial Congress.

Capital, therefore, is perfectly mobile in this new order, although invested in landed property, which runs no risk of being compromised by revolution or fraud, and which can in an instant be realised, without incurring any expense. Hence it is that the *rôles* of *proprietor* and of *capitalist* became synonymous in Harmony.

This mobility of capital is the point where civilised economists fail completely. In order to maintain capital mobile to-day, one runs so many risks that the English deposit with a banker, obtaining no interest and yet incurring the danger of bankruptcy, for the sole advantage of drawing their funds at pleasure. One may indeed keep one's capital mobile, in banks and commercial houses, by keeping one's self informed daily of the solvency of debtors ; but if we relax ever so little in our inquiries, we are implicated in failures, into which even the most cunning are surprised.

A Phalanx can never in any case become bankrupt, carry away its land, its palace, its workshops, its flocks. The district is, by its solidarity, an insurer against the ravages of the elements, which will be greatly reduced after five or six years of Harmony, that order causing an active climatic restoration. Fires will, likewise, become a matter of very inconsiderable consequence, owing to the excellent arrangements of this new domestic order.

A ward never incurs the risk of losing his capital, or of being wronged as regards management or income ; the administration is the same for him as it is for all the shareholders; if he has received shares in the different Phalanxes as a legacy, they are inscribed in the registers of those Phalanxes ; they bear the same interest there for him as for others, and cannot be abstracted from him under any pretext, until his majority, when he disposes of them himself.

A Phalanx may lose in a certain branch of endeavour, such as a new factory, but, before engaging in the undertaking, it gives every shareholder notice of any risky enterprise,—manufacturing, working a mine, or any other venture outside of the circle of familiar and customary operations. The shareholder is free to realise his shares, or to keep aloof from an enterprise in which he has no confidence. He can, then, by retaining his shares, limit himself to the usual chances ; in that case, he would obtain a full dividend, even though the Phalanx should have a smaller income through the failure of some novelty.

But a Phalanx *en masse*, directed by its Areopagus of experts, its Patriarchs, its neighbouring Cantons, and other skilled people, is not liable to imprudence like an individual, and where an industrial undertaking is in any degree adventurous, care is had to distribute the risk involved among a large number of Phalanxes, to deliberate a long time, to obtain insurance, etc. As to any risks from knavery, there can be none in Harmony.

I have remarked that every shareholder has the option of a fixed interest or of a contingent dividend of the proceeds of the year. The fixed interest has been estimated at $8\frac{1}{3}$ per cent. ; the contingent or associative dividend ought to yield more ; thus both the venturesome and the prudent may be satisfied.[1]— (U. U., iii., 451-453.)

The sense of ownership is the most powerful lever known, to electrify the civilised ; one may, without exaggeration, estimate the product of labour of an owner as double when compared with servile or wage labour. We see facts in proof of this every day ; workmen, shockingly slow and awkward when working for wages,

---

[1] The first savings, which are the most difficult, are admitted into the first grade of the industrial category, at 30 per cent. interest up to the amount of 1,000 francs, which constitutes a share ; the next succeeding savings will be received up to 1,000 francs at the rate of 28 per cent. ; the third at 18 per cent.

Why this enormous interest granted to the poor class ? because it is desired to imbue them at the very start with a spirit of ownership and saving, which are the source of good morals. By the end of the first month the value of the work of each individual, man, woman, or child, is known ; and what each one's share in the assets would be, deducting any advances made in food, clothing, housing ; one-twelfth will be offered them, providing they wish to deposit in the industrial bank at 30 per cent. ; all will agree to do so, for they are in possession of all that is necessary for maintenance and amusement,—gratuitous *fêtes* on Sundays, meals with fare raised from the third to the second degree, balls, etc.—(F. I. [Z], 7.)

become phenomena of diligence as soon as they labour on their own account.

The first problem, therefore, which ought to be studied in political economy is how to transform all wage-earners into co-interested or associated proprietors.—(U. U., iii., 171.)

A poor man, in Harmony, if he own but part of a share, but one-twentieth, is proprietor of the entire district, *in participation :* he can say, " our lands, our palace, our mansions, our forests, our works, our factories." All is his property ; he is interested in the whole of the personal and landed possessions.

If, under existing conditions, a forest is deteriorated, a hundred peasants will look upon it with indifference. The forest is simple property ; it belongs exclusively to the lord ; they rejoice at what may be prejudicial to him, and will secretly exert themselves to increase the damage. If a torrent sweeps the land away, three-fourths of the inhabitants own none along the banks, and laugh at the havoc. Frequently, they rejoice to see the water ravage the patrimony of a rich neighbour, whose property is simple, devoid of bonds of union with the body of the inhabitants, and inspiring them with no interest whatever.

In Harmony, where the interests are combined, and where each one is a partner, even if only to the extent of getting a share of the proceeds allotted to labour, each one always desires the prosperity of the whole district ; each one suffers from the harm which befals even the smallest portion of it. Thus, already through personal interest, good-will is general among the members, and this results solely from their not being wage-workers but co-interested ; knowing that any loss in the proceeds, be it but twelve groats, would take away five groats from those who, possessing neither money nor shares, have a part in the industrial dividend, arranged, as has already been observed, in three classes of dividends :

Five-twelfths for labour, four-twelfths for capital, three-twelfths for talent.

The dividend allotted to capital would give rise to jealousy among the masses of the people, if it were difficult for them to share in it.—(U. U., iii., 517.)

CHAPTER XIX

THE first right is the right to sustain life, to eat when one is hungry. This right is denied in civilisation by the philosophers, and conceded by Jesus Christ in these words :

" Have ye never read what David did, when he had need, and was an hungered, he, and they that were with him ? How he went into the house of God, and did eat the show-bread, which is not lawful to eat but for the priests, and gave also to them which were with him ? "

Jesus by these words consecrates the right of taking, WHEN ONE IS HUNGRY, what is necessary, where it may be found ; and this right imposes the duty upon the social body of securing to the people a minimum for maintenance ;—since civilisation deprives it of the first natural right, that of *the chase, fishing, gathering, pasturage*, it owes it an indemnity. As long as this duty is not recognised, there exists no social compact reciprocally agreed to ; there is nothing but a league of oppression, a league of the minority which possesses, against the majority which does not possess the necessaries of life, and which, for that reason, tends to resume the fifth right, to form clubs or internal leagues to despoil the possessors.—(F. I., 391.)

God has condemned man to earn his bread by the sweat of his brow ; but he did not condemn us to be deprived of the labour upon which our subsistence depends. We may, therefore, in virtue of the rights of man, bid Philosophy and Civilisation not to defraud us of the resource which God has bequeathed to us as a last resort and punishment, and to guarantee us at least a right to the species of labour to which we have been trained.

Labour is a cumulative right, resulting from the four cardinal rights : *the chase, fishing, gathering,* and *pasturage,* which tend to guarantee to us the active industry which Civilisation denies to us, or which it grants us upon ridiculous conditions, such as tributary labour, whose proceeds go to the master and not to the labourer.

We shall only get the equivalent of the four cardinal rights in a social order in which the poor man can say to his fellow-countryman, to his native phalanx : " I was born upon this land ; I demand admission to all classes of work practised here, a guarantee that I shall enjoy the fruit of my labour ; I demand that the instruments requisite to prosecute this labour be advanced to me, as well as maintenance, as a compensation for the right of stealing which Nature has given me." Every Harmonian, no matter how forlorn his condition, will always possess the right of addressing such language to his native place, and his demand will meet with a full acceptance.

It is only at such cost that humanity will really enjoy its rights : but in the present state, is it not insulting the poor to secure to them the rights of sovereignty, when they ask only the right to labour for the pleasures of the idle ?

We have, then, spent centuries in wrangling over the rights of man, without thinking of recognising the one which is the most essential, that of labour, without which the others are nothing.— (U. U., ii., 179.)

If the poor, the labouring class, are not happy in the associative state, they will disturb it by malevolence, robbery, rebellion ; such an order will fail in its object, which is to unite the passional with the material, to conciliate characters, tastes, instincts, and inequalities of every description.

Having charge of the accounts, the Administration advances to every poor member clothing, food, housing, for a year. They run no risk by this advance, because they know that the work the poor man will accomplish, *through attraction and as a scheme of pleasure,* will exceed in amount the sum of the advances made him ; and that, after the inventory is taken, the Phalanx will, in settling its accounts, find itself a debtor of the entire poor class to whom it shall have given this advance of the minimum, comprising :

Board at tables of the third class, five meals a day ;

A decent suit, and clothes for work and for occasions, as well as all the implements for husbandry and manufacture ;

Individual lodgings, consisting of a room and a closet, and admission to the public halls, the *fêtes* of the third class, and to plays in third class loges.—(U. U., iii., 445.)

But the first condition is *to invent and organise a régime of industrial attraction*.   Without this precaution, how can we think of guaranteeing the poor man a minimum ?   It would be accustoming him to slothfulness : he readily persuades himself that the minimum is a debt rather than an assistance, and he therefore concludes to remain in idleness.   That is what one remarks in England, where the tax of 150 millions for the needy serves only to increase their number ; so true is it that Civilisation is but a vicious circle, even in its most laudable actions.   What the people need is not alms, but work, attractive enough for the multitude to wish to devote to it even the days and hours reserved for idleness.

If political science knew the secret of bringing this lever into play, the minimum could *really be secured* by the absolute cessation of idleness.   The only ones remaining to be provided for would be the infirm ; a very light burden, and one not felt by the social body, if it became opulent and, through attraction, were relieved of slothfulness, and of indifferent labour, which is almost as sterile as slothfulness.—(U. U., ii., 172.)

Whatever their degree of well-being, the people would soon relapse into destitution if they multiplied without limit, like the populace of civilisation, the swarms of England, France, Italy, China, Bengal, etc.   It is necessary, therefore, to discover a means of security against the indefinite increase of population.[1]—(N. M., 10.)

[1] See chap. xxiii., *De la Population.*

CHAPTER XX

THE forms and direction of luxury vary according to the social periods. In barbarism, the fourth period, it is the body that is adorned ;—an Algerian is decked in gold ; he appears to be a Crœsus ; but if we visit his hut, we find his furniture inferior to that of a civilised artisan. The civilised, on the contrary, indulge in luxury only in their buildings, furniture, banquets, equipages ; in spite of their wealth, they are sometimes clad worse than their valets.

It is evident, therefore, that luxury changes its form and direction according to the different periods, and that, by passing from the fifth period or civilisation to the more advanced periods, the sixth, seventh, eighth, luxury might assume a direction entirely different from those which civilised usages have given it.

The luxury of Harmony, or the eighth period, is corporative ; each one is anxious to give brilliance to the groups and Series which he favours. We see a germ of this inclination in certain existing bodies ;—frequently a rich colonel will indulge in expense, in order to give distinction to his regiment through music, decorations ; and this commander will perhaps be very careless regarding his own dress, though spending a great deal upon the decoration of a thousand of his inferiors.—(U. U., iii., 536-537.)

Every corporate body is proud. Our customs have made pride a capital vice. The passionate Series will make a capital virtue of it, a civic virtue, from which they will derive, among other advantages, that of stimulating the rivalry of the workers, and the perfection of products.

If corporate bodies, even in civilisation, are averse to the appearance of poverty, it may readily be conceived that in Harmony they are averse even to the appearance of mediocrity.

The government of a Phalanx furnishes every group with all that is necessary to secure extreme neatness ; but the wealthy members add to this according to their vanity and their generosity.

Lucullus is captain of the group of red bigarreaux, and Scaurus of the group of brown bigarreaux.   These two rivals, in order to sustain the rivalry, commit just such follies as does a prince for his villa.   They have waggons and sheds constructed for the groups, more elegant than the paraphernalia of our operas. Each of them has a magnificent pavilion erected, at his own expense, in the centre of the rows of cherry-trees, in place of the modest shed which had been provided by the government.

That is why a sect or passionate Series is always resplendent with ornaments and equipages, whether at work or in pageants.   These gifts of the wealthy members are accepted, not as favours, but as a liberality which conduces to the relief of the corporation and of its industrial branch, to the maintenance of its rivalry with other Phalanxes.—(U. U., iii., 536-537.)

A like emulation will prevail among the Series of every description.   It is sufficient for a rich man to make any of them shine, to incite all the neighbouring districts to vie with it in some shape, if not in luxury, at least in neatness, in perfection.   This mania will seize all people of great means ; it will cause luxury to be expended upon labour and workshops, so repulsive to-day by their poverty, coarseness, and filth.

This pomp of labour will be an *industrial saving*, for it will help to inspire in children, as well as in their parents, a love for the exercise of productive industry.   Then everyone, instead of employing his superfluous wealth in constructing private mansions, which would be useless in Harmony, will spend his money in building fine workshops, fine terraces, fine sheds, for his favourite sects.

This effect, which is general in the mechanism of the passionate Series, gives luxury a productive direction.   Luxury in Harmony is applied to labour, the sciences, the arts, and notably to the kitchen.   Luxury conspires, along with a number of other causes, to render these occupations attractive to the child as well as the adult. The child will, in its infancy, take pleasure in going through all the workshops of its Phalanx, in initiating itself in the work of every miniature workshop, acquiring dexterity, strength, and practical knowledge, and becoming, however rich he may be, a producer qualified to do the actual work as well as to direct it.—(U. U., iii., 546.)

The luxury of the Harmonians amounts to next to nothing in various departments to which we uselessly devote enormous sums. In order to house Lucullus, Rome has to construct a huge palace : he will be contented in Harmony with three or four rooms because, in this new order, intercourse through the Series is too active to allow one time to stay in one's dwelling.

Everyone is always in the Seristeries, or public halls, the workshops, the fields, the stables ; they do not remain at home except in case of sickness or for a rendezvous ; it suffices, then, to have a bedroom and a boudoir ; the richest person's apartment, accordingly, has hardly more than three rooms.

Courtesy in Harmony differs absolutely from ours ; they do not pay useless visits, which would consume valuable time ; they see each other at meals, in the industrial groups, on 'Change, at evening entertainments. An outsider visits his friends at their industrial gatherings. Do you wish to pay Lucullus a visit flattering to him ? Seek him in the midst of the cherryists, in the group of the red bigarreaux, whose captain he is, in the orchard where he is at work and in his working-clothes ; at the close of the session, you will breakfast or lunch with him and his group, in the superb mansion built, at his expense, and on the façade of which the group has had the following inscription engraved :

Ex munificentia Luculli, Cerasorum clarissimi sectatoris.

It is here that he lavishes his pomp, and that he loves to excite admiration for the work of his colleagues, over whom he presides.

Thus the usages and the policy of Harmony bring to bear upon productive industry all the brilliancy, all the aid, of that luxury which to-day is attached only to unproductive functions, leaving agriculture and the workshop in the most abject wretchedness.— (U. U., iii., 539-541.)

We shall find among the Harmonians a policy totally contrary to our ideas of commerce, which promote waste and the changes of fashion, under the pretext of maintaining the workman. But in Harmony the workman, the agriculturist, and the consumer, are one and the same person; he has no interest in practising extortion upon himself, as in civilisation, where everyone strives to promote industrial disturbance occasioned by changes of fashion, and to manufacture poor goods or poor furniture, in order to double consumption, to enrich the merchants at the expense of the people and of real wealth.

They will calculate, in Harmony, that changes of fashion, defective quality, or imperfect workmanship, would cause a loss of five hundred francs per individual, for the poorest of the Harmonians possesses a wardrobe of clothes for all seasons, and is accustomed to using furniture, trappings, and appurtenances, for work or pleasure, of a fine quality.

They do not calculate thus in civilisation, because that society, in industry as in everything, is inclined to duplicity or internal warfare. Its industry is a veritable civil war of the producer against the idler, whom he tries to plunge into ruin; and of the merchant against the social body, which he incites to dupery. The science which applauds this conflict resembles a senseless master who should incite his domestics to break quantities of dishes and furniture, for the benefit of the manufacturers. Everything is but political madness, as long as the interest of the individual is not bound up with the interest of the mass.— (U. U., 575.)

Let us refute a strange sophism of the economists who maintain that the unlimited increase of manufactured products is an increase of wealth; the consequence of that would be, that if every person could be induced to use four times as many clothes as he does, the social world would attain to four times its present wealth in manufactured products.

No truth whatever in this; their calculation is as false on this point as it is on the desirability of unlimited increase of population, or *food for cannon*. Real wealth, in Harmony, is based upon:

The greatest possible consumption of varieties of food ;

The smallest possible consumption of varieties of clothing and furniture.

Variety, applied to both kinds of consumption, demands the maximum on one side and the minimum on the other, all harmony being based upon direct and inverse action of impulses.

This principle has escaped civilised economists, who, likening manufactures to agriculture, have believed that excessive manufacturing and consumption of goods is a measure of the increase of wealth. The speculations of Harmony upon this point are the reverse ; it desires, in clothing and in furniture, *infinite variety*, but the *smallest consumption*.

When I was little practised in the calculations of attraction, and I began to balance the portions and the results, in every branch of industry, I was greatly astonished to find that, strictly analysed, there was little attraction for manufacturing labour, and that the associative order, while creating agricultural allurements in unlimited quantities, would develop only an insignificant amount of manufacturing allurements. This result seemed inconsistent to me, opposed to what necessity demanded. Little by little, I perceived that, in accordance with the principle of attractions proportioned to ends, God ought to have restricted the allurements of manufacture, by reason of the excellence of associative industry, which raises every manufactured article to the acme of perfection, so that furniture and clothing attain prodigious durability, become *everlasting*.

Shoes made by a fashionable shoemaker of Paris will go into holes without fail after a month's wear ; and this is as it should be ; for that shoemaker would compromise his art, *if he should furnish common people who go about on foot.* The shoes coming from the workshops of a Phalanx will be in good condition at the end of ten years, because two conditions, unknown in the present order, will have been fulfilled :

Excellence of material and of workmanship ;

Fitness for its purpose and for durability.

These details, sordid in appearance, become sublime when one considers that they are capable of securing an *annual* saving of 400 milliards in wearing apparel, and 2,000 milliards in the total loss which would be incurred if the Harmonians failed to take combined saving into their calculations.

With them, economy becomes *bon ton*, through the influence of the combined action of the four tones. The Harmonians, though liberal and fond of elegance, have a passion, as being *bon ton*, for savings which we regard as niggardliness, sordid avarice, such as the picking up of a pin or using the other end of a match. They will treat you profusely to the finest dishes, and regard you as a vandal if you waste a cherry-seed or the skin of an apple.

With us, as a matter of propriety, one writes to the minister upon paper of ample dimensions, three-fourths of which is useless, and the minister, by way of fiscal parade, replies with two lines upon a sheet a yard long. A contrary spirit will prevail among the Harmonians, and, in writing to the minister, honesty will demand that the smallest quantity of paper possible shall be used. To fail to do that would be to offend the minister, to suppose him indifferent to small savings, which in Harmony are the guarantee of social happiness, not only on account of the annual gain of 2,000 milliards, but on account of maintaining the equilibrium between services and attractions. This equilibrium would be destroyed, if an excessive consumption of manufactured articles were to divert people from the pleasant agricultural sessions, and oblige them to take hours from such labour and devote them to manufacture, whose allurements are limited in quantity, while agricultural Attraction is unlimited.

In an order in which all classes will be linked by ties of affection, potentates themselves will be found to set the fashion in that economy of clothes which we characterise as a sordid spirit, and which is the real spirit of God, whose first quality is the economy of means. God does not waste an atom in the mechanism of the universe, and everywhere where there is an absence of general economy, we may say there is an absence of the spirit of God.—(U. U., iii., 209-210.)

CHAPTER XXI

OF THE FUSION OF CLASSES

THERE are sixteen classes in civilisation, not including slavery ; a corporative hatred is found prevailing between all these classes ; the civilised order with all its talk about the charming fraternity of intercourse, and about morality, creates only a labyrinth of discords, which may be distinguished into :

An ascending scale of hatred;

A descending scale of contempt.

If we see in civilisation some gleams of a fusion of castes, as in Naples, where the nobility patronise the lazzaroni ; in Spain, where the rich clergy patronise the beggars ; this alliance of extreme castes is only a source of evil, the civilised state creating only subversive and mischievous unions,—whether in love, where intimate intercourse between men of the higher classes and women of the people constitutes only germs of confusion, through the birth of bastards, or through unequal marriages, which are the cause of dissensions in families ; or in ambition, where the wealthy class does not come into close contact with the people, except to manipulate some intrigue baneful to the public peace, affairs of party, leagues for oppression.—(N. M., 324-325.)

It is among children that friendship can assume full sway : in them it is not opposed by cupidity, by love, or by interest in the family. Friendship in the early years would confound all ranks, did not parents intervene by cultivating sentiments of pride in their children.

In the period of adolescence, love steps in to confound ranks and puts a king upon a level with the shepherdess whom he woos. We have, then, even under existing conditions, germs of fusion of the unequal classes; we find them even in ambition: it accustoms a superior to mingle familiarly with his inferior, in party concerns, in electoral intrigues. The Scipios and the Catos have been known to meet a boor and press his hand in order to gain his vote; to what mean acts do the English lords resort, to capture a "rotten borough," paying dearly for it at the same time !

We have, then, in the present state, many germs tending to initiate the fusion of classes, but by ways that are abject, by sordid cupidity. We already see, through these base means, a closer mingling between people belonging to classes averse to each other; such intercourse will be rendered twenty times easier when people will use noble means, be actuated by genuine ties of affection.—(N. M., 278.)

All liberty would become a germ of dissension, so long as the high and the low should hate each other as they do to-day. The sole means of uniting them passionally, of interesting them in each other, is to unite them in industry. The farmers who have a share in the harvest wish the portion allotted to the master to be plentiful, so that theirs may increase in proportion to the yield; for if the master gets little grain on account of the poor harvest, the farmers get little when the social distribution is made.

The secret of the *unity of interest*, therefore, lies in Association. The three classes, being associated and united in interest, would forget their hatred; and that the more readily because the opportunities for attractive labour would put an end to the drudgery of the people and the disdain of the rich for inferiors, whose labours, now become enticing, they would share. There would be an end to the envy with which the poor regard the idle, who reap without having sown: there would no longer be any idlers, or poor, and social antipathies would disappear with the causes which produced them.—(U. U., ii., 173.)

That which will charm a rich man in the associative state will be his ability to repose perfect confidence in all who surround him, to forget the cunning with which one must be armed at all points in the relations of civilisation, and yet be unable to escape dupery. In the Phalanx, a rich man, going in with unlimited confidence, will have no snares to fear, no importunate demands to trouble him, because the Harmonians, provided with a sufficient *minimum,* have nothing in the way of personal interest to ask of anyone, assured as they are of obtaining, in every branch of attractive industry, a compensation proportioned to their labour, their capacity, and their capital, if they have any. One of their prized possessions is the absence of patronage, the certainty that all patronage would be useless to their rivals as well as to themselves, that compensation and advancement will be equitably distributed, in spite of all intrigues.

Intimacies among those who are unequal will, therefore, be very readily formed in Harmony : the reunions will allure people by the gaiety, the well-being, the civility, and the integrity of the lower classes, by the elegance of the industrial arrangements, and the harmony of the members. The poorest will be proud of their new condition, of the high destiny of their phalanx, which will change the aspect of the world ; they will be anxious to distinguish themselves from the civilised by a probity, a justice, which will be the only avenues of profit. They will in a short time have adopted the spirit and the manners that are assumed by those whom a stroke of fortune transports suddenly from a cottage to a mansion ; and this *bon ton* will be very readily appropriated by the lower class of the first phalanx, if it be taken from regions where the people are refined, such as the environs of Tours and of Paris. [1]

It will be partly through their hatred of the masses in civilisation, that the rich will from the very start grow enamoured of those of the Phalanx ; they will regard them as men of a different species, and cultivate familiarity with them, through increased

[1] Let us take a parvenu installed in a mansion ; these parvenus are not stimulated by a frank and friendly criticism, such as will prevail in the industrial groups ; they are, on the contrary, flattered, deceived by all who surround them ; this sycophancy greatly retards their refinement. But in the associative order, where everyone acquires a taste for *bon ton*, the people, by the aid of friendly irony, will be able to attain polished manners much more rapidly than parvenus, to whom no one dares to address a remonstrance.

horror of civilised grossness and deceit.   They will forget their station as readily among the people in Harmony, as they do to-day with the polished grisettes, who, nevertheless, belong to the common people, but assume fine manners.

I calculate, therefore, that fusion will be inaugurated from the second month ; that the wealthy class will be the first to feel indignant at this principle of civilised policy : *there must be many poor people in order that there may be some rich ones;* a principle that will very soon be replaced by this one : *the poor must be in the enjoyment of graduated ease, in order that the rich may be happy.*

Let us remember that one of the principal means of effecting this fusion will be the progress of children in natural education, or the incitement to labour and study through pleasure, without any impetus from parents or teachers.—(N. M., 279-280.)

CHAPTER XXII

OF DUTIES TOWARDS ANIMALS

ANIMALS are happy in Harmony through the gentleness and the unity of the methods employed in managing them, the choice and the variety of food, the care of the passionate members, who observe all the precautions calculated to improve the various species : none of this attention can be bestowed in our brutal civilisation, which cannot make even the stables comfortable. We may assert without exaggeration that the asses in Harmony will be much better housed and better kept than the peasants of the beautiful land of France.—(U. U., iv., 92.)

Is it not sinking beneath the level of the lower animals, to ignore the consideration we owe to their instincts? They are profitable to us only in so far as we secure their well-being. The Little Hordes exercise supreme police power in regard to the animal kingdom : whoever should ill-treat quadruped, bird, insect, either by using them roughly or by making them suffer in the shambles, would be amenable to the divan of the Little Hordes ; and, no matter what his age, he would find himself arraigned before a tribunal of children, as being inferior in reason to the children themselves. For it is a maxim in Harmony, that, animals being profitable only in so far as they are well treated, he who abuses these creatures, unable to avenge themselves, is himself more of a beast than the beast that he persecutes. —(U. U., iv., 155.)

1 In our perfectible civilisation, people strive to refine upon the sufferings of animals, saying why are they oxen, why are they chickens, why are they fish? The butcher drags them by the aid of the lash and the bites of dogs into shambles reeking with blood, the smell of which infuriates them, and makes them suffer death by anticipation. Every cook will burst out laughing if he is asked to kill or stupefy a fish before scaling and opening it.

A truth which is quite unknown up to the present is that domestic animals are creatures capable of regulated harmony, and that their training cannot become profitable to man except in so far as they are raised in accordance with that method.   Here is a scheme for colossal enrichment; it is well worthy of the attention of an age which, more than any other, gauges everything by its weight in gold.—(U. U., iv., 84.)

Among quadrupeds, there is scarcely a twentieth which ally themselves to us, excluding the negative species, such as the stag, the deer, the roe, which, without being useful to us, contribute to our pleasures ;

Among birds, scarcely a hundredth allied to us.

Among insects, scarcely a millionth.

It is, then, a creation subversive of the laws of harmony ; allied to those laws only by slender ties, forming exceptions, or the transition between the present evil and the future good.   These useful animals are an illustration of the system which will fully prevail in the approaching creations, where at least seven-eighths of the quadrupeds and birds will be found to be the allies of man,— such as the bee, the cochineal, the kermes, the silk-worm are to-day.—(M., 77.)

The series of Harmonian butchers will refine upon the precautions which may spare animals the idea of death.   They will take care to have the slaughter-house cleansed by a conduit and perfumed ; the animals will be fastened in a body, so that the group of slaughterers may strike them simultaneously : they will, in short, take all the precautions which may spare them real or imaginary suffering.   The details of these attentions would appear ridiculous in the eyes of the French, who everywhere delight in torturing animals,—quadrupeds, birds, fish, even to butterflies.   The affection of the Harmonians for the brute creation lends great prominence to the duties of a butcher intelligent in managing them, and this calling is classed in the first rank in necessity.—(U. U., iv., 519.)

CHAPTER XXIII

OF THE EQUILIBRIUM OF POPULATION

AMONG the inconsistencies and the blunders of modern policy, there is nothing more shocking than the neglect to legislate upon the equilibrium of population, upon the proportion of the number of consumers to the productive forces. It were vain to discover the means of increasing the product four or even five-fold, if the human race were condemned to multiply as it does to-day ; constantly to accumulate a mass of people, three or four times as great as that to which it ought to be limited in order to maintain the graduated comfort of the different classes.

In every age, the equilibrium of population has been the stumbling-block, or one of the stumbling-blocks, of civilised policy. Already the ancients, who had so many uncultivated regions around them which could be colonised, found no other remedy for the exuberance of population than to tolerate the exposure and destruction of infants, the killing of superfluous slaves,—which was resorted to by the virtuous Spartans,—or having them perish in naumachies for the amusement of Roman citizens, proud of the fine name of free men, but very far removed from filling the *rôle* of just men.

More recently, we have seen modern politicians confess their discomfiture regarding the problem of population. I have quoted Stewart, Wallace, and Malthus, the only writers worthy of attention upon this subject, because they acknowledge the helplessness of science. Their wise views upon the vicious circle of population are stifled by economic jugglers, who shove aside this problem as they do so many others. Stewart, more honest, has treated it very well in his hypothesis of an island, which, being well cultivated, was able to support 1,000 inhabitants of unequal fortune, in comfort ; but, says he, if the population swells to 3,000 and 4,000 ; to 10,000 and 20,000, how is it to be supported ?

The answer given is, that colonisation must be resorted to, multitudes of people sent away; this is to quibble with the question ; for if the entire globe were inhabited, peopled to the full, whither could the swarms of colonists be sent?

The sophists answer, that the globe is not all peopled, and will not be so very soon ; that is one of the subterfuges of the Owen sect, which, promising happiness, evades the problem of the equilibrium of population, and says that it will take at least 300 years for the earth to be peopled to its FULL CAPACITY. They are mistaken ; it will take only 150 years. However that be, it is retreating before a problem to relegate its solution to the future, 300 years hence, and without guaranteeing that the solution will be found then. Besides, granting that it would be 300 years before the earth were fully peopled, such a theory would still be a very imperfect one,—the theory of a happiness or pretended happiness which should disappear at the end of 300 years through a defect in social policy, through the exuberance of population.

Now, as it is certain that this scourge will not tarry 300 years and that it will appear at the end of 150 years,—under the conditions of universal peace and general plenty which will be brought about by the associative state,—the scheme of this new order must provide very effective means to prevent excess of population, to reduce the number of inhabitants of the globe to a just proportion between means and needs—to about 5 milliards, without the danger of seeing the population increase to 6, 7, 8, 10, 12 milliards ; an exuberance which would be inevitable should the entire globe introduce the civilised *régime*.

Nature, in the associative state, sets up four dikes against excess of population; these are :

1° The vigour of women.

2° The gastrosophic *régime*.

3° Phanerogamic morals.

4° Integral exercise.

1° *Vigour :* we see the effect of this now among women *of the city ;* out of four that are barren, three are robust, while the delicate women are fertile to an excessive and vexatious degree. The barren ones are generally those whom one would have believed the most likely to bear children. It will be answered that in the country the robust women are not barren ; I know it, and it is an additional evidence in favour of the natural method, which operates *by a linking of the four means applied in combination,* and not by the isolated employment of any one of the four.

2° *The gastrosophic régime :* Whence this difference in fecundity in favour of robust peasants ? It is the result of an abstemious life, of coarse food, limited to vegetables. Women in the cities have delicate fare,—that is one means towards sterility, which will become more powerful in Harmony, where every person is a refined gastronome. Thus combining the extreme vigour of the Harmonian women with the delicate fare which they will enjoy, we have already two means of promoting sterility. I pass briefly over objections the examination of which would fill an article larger than this ; it must be borne in mind that this is a summary.[1]

3° *Phanerogamic morals.*[2]

4° *Integral exercise* distributed over all the physical faculties, by means of short sessions and change of occupation. No attention has ever been paid to the effects produced upon puberty and fecundity by difference in bodily exercise ; the contrasts in this particular are striking : we see villagers attaining puberty much later than residents of cities or children of rich country people. If bodily exercise is integral, extended alternately and proportionately over all parts of the body, the organs of generation are developed later ; we have a proof of this in the

---

[1] For the rest, after three generations of Harmony, two-thirds of the women will be unfruitful, as is the case with all flowers which, by the refinements of cultivation, have been raised to a high degree of perfection. —(F. I., 560.)

[2] See chap. v., *Of the Condition of Women.*

children of princes, who marry at fourteen years of age, while villagers are often not marriageable at sixteen.

When the four means, set forth above, shall be employed *in combination*, the chances of fecundity and sterility will be the reverse of what they are at present; that is to say, that instead of excess of population, the only thing to be feared will be a *deficit;* and measures will be taken to stimulate that fecundity which every prudent man dreads to-day. The man of sense does not wish to have more than a few children, so as to assure them the fortune which is indispensable to happiness; the man devoid of sense and given over to carnal indulgence, begets children by the dozen, like Feth-Ali, Shah of Persia, who excused himself upon the ground that *it is God who sends them, and there are never too many honest men.* God wishes, on the contrary, to limit their number proportionately to the means of subsistence; and the social man lowers himself to the level of insects by bringing into the world a swarm of children who will be reduced to devouring each other through excess of numbers. They will not consume each other bodily like insects, fish, and wild beasts; but they will devour each other politically, through rapine, wars, and the perfidies of perfectible civilisation.—(N. M., 335-338.)

THE END